What the critics are saying about
The Best of the British Virgin Islands, Second Edition
and Pamela Acheson's writing:

"If you want to see the real British Virgin Islands, this book is for you...offers a near-guarantee of a great trip."
—*Independent Publisher*

"*The Best of the British Virgin Islands* is essential to getting the most out of any trip to the British Virgin Islands."
—*Midwest Book Review*

"Pamela Acheson shares her intimate knowledge of hotels, inns, bars, restaurants, shops and attractions."
—*Virgin Islands Weekly Journal*

"A wonderful and lighthearted guidebook...full of insider tips and recommendations."
—*Essentially America*

"Unquestionably the best guidebook ever written on the British Virgin Islands."
—*Peter Island Morning Sun*

"A valid and nifty guide to wonderful places."
—*The Naples Daily News*

"Acheson does a lot of footwork for her readers."
—*The Observer*

Pamela Acheson is one "of our extraordinary writers."
—*Fodor's Caribbean*

THE BEST
OF THE
BRITISH VIRGIN
ISLANDS

Second Edition

PAMELA ACHESON

TWO THOUSAND THREE ASSOCIATES
TTTA

Published by
TWO THOUSAND THREE ASSOCIATES
4180 Saxon Drive, New Smyrna Beach, FL 32169
Tel: 1-800-598-5256

Copyright © 1998, 2000 by Pamela Acheson

Acheson, Pamela.
     The best of the British Virgin Islands / Pamela Acheson . — 2nd
ed.
          p.   cm.
     ISBN 0-9639905-4-3
- 1. British Virgin Islands—Guidebooks.   I. Title
 F2129.A63   1997
 917.297'2504--dc21   97-44960
                                                                        CIP

Printed in the United States of America

Photo Credits
Front Cover: Pamela Acheson. Looking across Sir Francis Drake Channel to Tortola.
Back Cover: Bob Krist. Deep Bay Beach at Biras Creek Resort on Virgin Gorda.

ISBN 0-9639905-4-3

Third Printing December 2000

For Auntie Bea

TABLE OF CONTENTS

SPECIAL FEATURES

"Silver bird fly me away
to where the winter's warm
and the sea breezes
blow through the night"
—*from* Island Blues
by Quito Rhymer

ACKNOWLEDGEMENTS
To Samantha, for her great advice and generational point of view, and to my husband, for his all-encompassing support, patience, advice, and on-going contributions, editorially and otherwise.

DISCLAIMER
The author has made every effort to ensure accuracy in this book. Neither the author nor the publisher is responsible for anyone's traveling experiences.

INTRODUCTION

The Best of the British Virgin Islands, Second Edition, is a labor of love. I have been traveling to the Virgin Islands for over 30 years and have been a resident of the British Virgin Islands for much of the past decade.

I have had the pleasure of watching many repeat visitors fall in love with the BVI just the way I did. I wrote this book to try to help every visitor — even the first time visitor — enjoy the very best these wonderful islands have to offer.

You'll notice some special features in the book called "Things you wished you had known sooner." Well, in a way, that is what this whole book is all about. I hope my years of island experiences not only offer the very best of the BVI to the reader, but also help everyone avoid the possible pitfalls and problems of traveling to an unfamiliar place.

The book is arranged alphabetically by island, and covers everything, from places to stay to restaurants and snorkel trips. I hope it helps you make educated decisions on everything from where to go, what to do, and how to have the most fun — for you. An appendix in the back of the book provides ferry schedules and other practical information.

The British Virgin Islands are special. I hope when you visit you leave your footprints on dozens of deserted beaches and bring home many special memories.

Enjoy them and have fun!

— *P.A.*

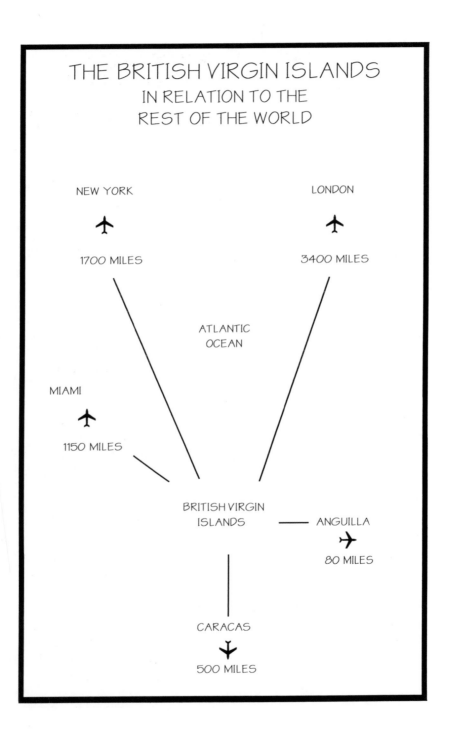

THE BRITISH VIRGIN ISLANDS
IN RELATION TO THE
REST OF THE WORLD

NEW YORK

1700 MILES

LONDON

3400 MILES

ATLANTIC
OCEAN

MIAMI

1150 MILES

BRITISH VIRGIN
ISLANDS — ANGUILLA

80 MILES

CARACAS

500 MILES

1. THE BRITISH VIRGIN ISLANDS

What are they?
They are a stunningly beautiful collection of 50 or so islands, islets, and cays that, with the exception of Anegada, are incredibly close together. Most are mountainous and steep-sided, some are rocky, and all are fringed with numerous white-sand, crescent-shaped beaches. Except for the coral atoll of Anegada, all are volcanic in origin.

Where are they?
In the Caribbean, about 1700 miles southeast of New York City and about 1150 miles southeast of Miami. They are 60 miles east of Puerto Rico and about 80 miles slightly northwest of Anguilla. Sombrero, an uninhabited island, sits halfway between the BVI and Anguilla.

Where are the BVI in relation to the USVI?
Right next to each other! The British Virgin Islands and the U.S. Virgin Islands share the same archipelago: the USVI have the western half and the BVI the eastern half, with some overlapping in the middle. In places, shorelines of the USVI and BVI lie less than half a mile apart.

How are the BVI different from the USVI?
Despite the close shorelines, stepping into the BVI from the USVI is like traveling to a far away country. The atmosphere is completely different. The population of the USVI is over 100,000 and two million tourists head there annually. Only 18,000 people live in all of the BVI.

The BVI is an entire country where almost everyone knows everyone else. Resorts are small. There isn't a lot of nightlife. Although there is plenty of good food, there are only a handful of sophisticated restaurants. It's not a shopper's haven but there are wonderful things to buy. It's quiet and remote and the U.S. seems a million miles away.

What can you do in the BVI?

Walk deserted, dazzling, white-sand beaches. Drive to spectacular mountaintop vistas. Swim, snorkel, and dive in astonishingly clear, calm water. Horseback ride. Hike in the mountains. Sail in exceptionally protected waters. Go deep sea fishing. Windsurf (locals travel island to island this way!). Or learn to do any of these things. You can also relax, or read, or rest. Or just sit very still and look around you.

The BVI offer peace, quiet, and a slower pace. The BVI people are warm and friendly. These are the islands to come for uninhabited beaches. Deserted snorkeling places. Bays where no one else is anchored. This is a place you can take in at your own speed, without crowds of other people blocking your view.

What's special about the BVI?

Everything! One of the BVI's greatest assets is its truly spectacular scenery. Above the water and below. There are breath-taking mountaintop panoramas, stunning sunrises and sunsets, beaches that will steal your heart, water in countless unreproducible shades of blue. Below the water line is another magnificent world. There are great wrecks to dive around. And scuba and snorkel areas so full of gaudily decorated fish that it will make you laugh.

Do the islands in the BVI differ from one another?

Absolutely! Despite the fact that the British Virgin Islands are lumped together as the "BVI," each island is actually very different, with its own unique character. When you've seen one, you definitely have not seen them all.

How easy is it to visit several British Virgin Islands?

The BVI is the only place in the entire Caribbean where so many islands are so close together. Many are only three or four miles from each other. Since it's all one country, it's incredibly easy to travel from island to island. Once you've cleared customs into the BVI, you are free to hop from one island to another — without paying departure and arrival taxes, going through customs, or lugging suitcases around. To get from island to island, you can go on a day sail, a group boat trip, rent your own little motor boat, or take a public ferry.

2. EACH ISLAND IN A NUTSHELL

All of the British Virgin Islands are hilly and close together except very flat and far-flung Anegada. All are wonderful but each one is unbelieveably different from the others. Each one has a character all its own.

Anegada is an eleven-mile long, flat coral atoll surrounded by reefs. It's the northernmost of the BVI and lies barely above sea level about 15 miles north of Virgin Gorda. Only 188 people live on the island. There are few places to stay and only a handful of extremely simple restaurants but there are miles of deserted beaches, great bone fishing and deep sea fishing, and some of the best snorkeling in the world.

Beef Island is just 600 feet off Tortola's East End and a short bridge connects the two islands. Beef Island is where the Tortola airport is actually located (which always confuses first-time visitors — "Why am I flying to Beef Island?") and it's also where the ferries are for Pusser's Marina Cay or Virgin Gorda's North Sound. It has a nice beach, a windsurfing school, some little stores, and several restaurants.

Cooper Island is five miles south of Tortola. It's a small island favored by the charter yacht crowd because of the large number of available moorings and the popular open-air restaurant. The island also has several inhabitants, some rental villas, and a simple 12-room inn.

Ginger Island is uninhabited and six miles southeast of Tortola.

Great Camanoe Island is just north of Beef Island and has a small number of residents.

Guana Island is a large private island just north of Tortola's East End and contains a private nature preserve and small resort.

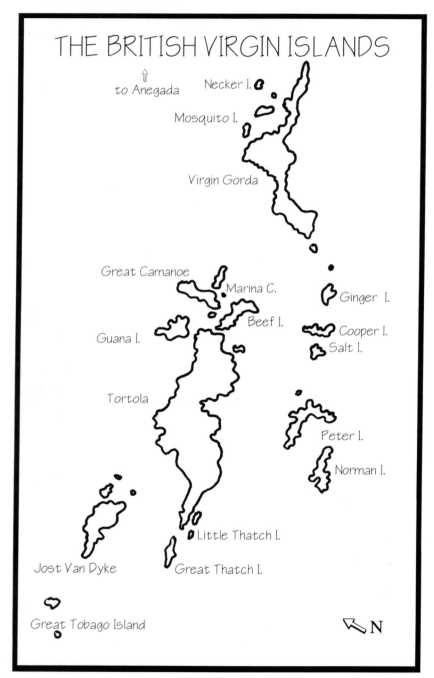

THE BRITISH VIRGIN ISLANDS

to Anegada

Necker I.

Mosquito I.

Virgin Gorda

Great Camanoe

Marina C.

Ginger I.

Beef I.

Cooper I.

Guana I.

Salt I.

Tortola

Peter I.

Norman I.

Little Thatch I.

Jost Van Dyke

Great Thatch I.

Great Tobago Island

N

Jost Van Dyke is a hilly four mile long island four miles northwest of Tortola with 163 inhabitants and beach front restaurants and bars. Two excellent anchoring harbors and Foxy's famous Tamarind Bar have made the island a "must stop" for just about everyone. There are very few places to stay overnight, but it's a really great day-trip.

Marina Cay is just north of Beef Island. Although it's barely larger than a rock, it's home to tiny Marina Cay Resort, Marina Cay Restaurant, and a Pusser's Store, plus 35 moorings just offshore.

Mosquito Island is a half-mile square private island just north of Virgin Gorda that borders North Sound. It's the location of Drake's Anchorage, a small resort, and there are several lovely beaches.

Necker Island is a luxurious private retreat a mile and a half north of Virgin Gorda.

Norman Island is five miles south of Tortola and is uninhabited (except for several herds of goats). It's a favorite anchoring spot and has a floating restaurant, The William Thornton, anchored offshore.

Peter Island is a four and a half mile long, private island five miles south of Tortola with a 50-room resort nestled against its north shore. Ferry service is available from just outside Road Town for those wishing to use the beaches or dine there.

Salt Island is four miles south of Tortola. This island's salt pond used to be the BVI's source of salt and older residents remember boating over here to pick up the family's salt supply. A family still lives here but there are no public facilities.

Scrub Island is a bit east of Great Camanoe and has just a few residents.

Tortola is the largest, the hilliest, and by far the most populated of the BVI, with 15,388 people. Although quiet by U.S. standards, this is the busiest island in the BVI and has the BVI's only real town, Road Town. Stores, bars, restaurants, and pubs are clustered in Road Town and also scattered around the island. There are beautiful beaches along the north shore and miles of roads that are astonishingly steep in places but show off awesome views.

Virgin Gorda lies east of Tortola and is physically a third smaller. It has a population of only 2,834. There are a small number of resorts, shops, and restaurants at each end of the island. A single road, which runs up over one big mountain, connects the two ends. Virgin Gorda's southern end is flat and fairly arid with big boulders scattered about and there are a handful of resorts and a tiny town. At the north end is calm North Sound, an exceptionally protected body of water excellent for water sports. Four resorts, all but one accessible only by boat, are scattered along the hilly shores of North Sound.

West Seal Dog, East Seal Dog, George Dog, Great Dog, West Dog, Cockroach Island, Fallen Jerusalem, Round Rock, Dead Chest, Little Thatch, Great Thatch, The Indians, Pelican Island, Sandy Spit, Great Tobago, and **Little Tobago** are the delightful names of some of the uninhabited islands in the BVI. Many have stunning beaches and snorkeling spots and there are numerous opportunities to visit these uninhabited islands, either by renting your own little powerboat or hiring a captain or joining a group for a half day or a full day of beaching and snorkeling. Keep an eye out for the great names of points and bays, such as the "Inaccessibles" on Mosquito Island, or "Cow Wreck Beach" on Anegada.

> **"People see only what they are prepared to see."**
> *— Emerson*

3. ANEGADA

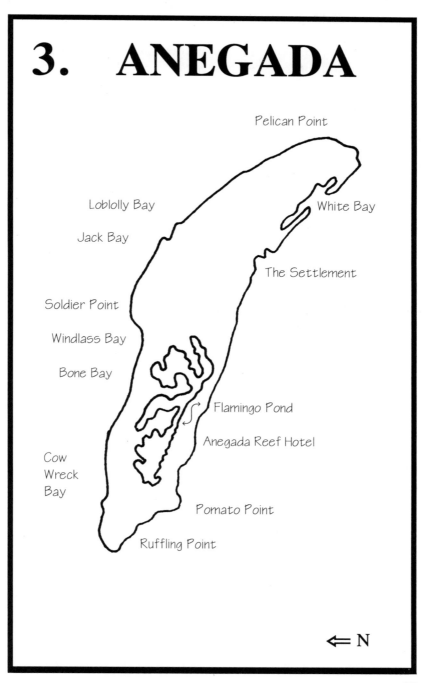

Pelican Point

Loblolly Bay

White Bay

Jack Bay

The Settlement

Soldier Point

Windlass Bay

Bone Bay

Flamingo Pond

Anegada Reef Hotel

Cow
Wreck
Bay

Pomato Point

Ruffling Point

⇐ N

ANEGADA

Anegada is a flat coral atoll sixteen miles north of Virgin Gorda which is almost entirely surrounded by treacherous reefs. Snorkelers and divers love Anegada but it's a sailor's nightmare. There are well over 300 wrecks just offshore. In fact, charter companies don't allow their boats to be taken to Anegada without a captain. The approach to the only two anchorages takes a great deal of skill and local knowledge.

There are just a few places to stay, a handful of simple restaurants, and miles of stunning white-sand beach. The island itself is not much to look at, but the underwater scenery is spectacular. Exquisite coral formations shimmering with colorful fish begin just inches from shore. You can snorkel here in very calm, clear water and swim to one coral grouping after another, for hours and hours.

Staying on Anegada is a remarkably relaxing experience. There is "nothing" to do. Take a picnic to a deserted area of beach or have lunch at a little beach restaurant. Spend the day snorkeling, or perhaps snoozing with a book in your lap. Or look for pink flamingoes in the salt ponds. Dine on delicious local lobster.

Anegada is also a place to come for excellent deep-sea fishing and bone fishing. The island is a great stop for a week or a day. You can fly here from Tortola in ten minutes or you can take a boat trip from Tortola or Virgin Gorda.

GETTING THERE
Clair Aero Services (495-2271) flies between Beef Island/Tortola and Anegada on Mondays, Wednesdays, Fridays, and Sundays. Flights leave Beef Island at 8 am and 5 pm and leave Anegada at 8:20 am and 5:20 pm. The round-trip fare is $59 per person.

GETTING THERE FOR THE DAY
Fly BVI (495-1747) has a package trip for $125 per person, minimum of two, that includes a tour of the island and lunch. For boat trips to Anegada see Boat Trips from Tortola (page 70), Boat Trips from Virgin Gorda (page 102 and 110), or call Speedy's (495-5240). The flight schedule for **Clair Aero Services** (above) also works well for a full day on Anegada.

GETTING AROUND
Tony's Taxi (495-8027) will take you on a tour or drop you at a beach. **DW Jeep Rental** (495-9677) rents vehicles. If there's no answer, try after 5 pm.

RESTAURANTS
Anegada Reef Hotel (495-8002) cooks up great grilled lobster, chicken, and fish dinners which are served by candlelight.

Big Bamboo (495-2019) is right on beautiful Loblolly Bay beach near Jack Bay Point. It's the place to come for a sweet Anegada lobster, Jamaican jerk chicken, and local conch or grilled snapper. *Lunch only. Dinner by request.*

Cow Wreck Beach Bar and Grill (495-9461), beachfront at Lower Cow Wreck Beach, serves lobster grilled or in sandwiches, fish, and burgers.

Dotsy's Bakery and Sandwich Shop (495-9667) bakes breads, muffins, pies, and cookies and serves burgers, fish and chips, and pizza. *Open 9 am to 7 pm.*

Flash of Beauty (495-8014) is a simple beach bar at Loblolly Bay East serving fresh Anegada lobster, grilled fish, or sandwiches. *Open 10 am to 9 pm.*

SHOPPING
Anegada Reef Hotel Boutique (495-8002) showcases stylish resortwear, local spices and relishes, island prints, original soaps, and excellent gift items.

Pam's Kitchen and Bakery (495-9237) bakes breads, muffins, pies, cookies, rolls, and even pizza. Salsas, hot sauces, jams, and soaps are for sale, too.

Pat's Pottery and Art (495-8031) features mugs, plates and platters, pitchers, and bowls all whimsically hand-painted in pastel colors.

WHERE TO STAY
Anegada Reef Hotel is a wonderful, informal hotel run by Lowell and Sue Wheatley. Rooms are on the spare side, but it's the atmosphere that counts here. It's just so delightfully laid back. If the bartender is not around, you make a drink and write down what you had. Meal hours, special trips, and messages are casually scribbled on a blackboard daily. The hotel is on a strand of sand on the south side of the island, but snorkelers (bring your equipment, no rentals) and beach lovers will want to spend their days on the deserted and gorgeous beach that runs for miles along the island's spectacular north shore. *16 rooms. $275 a night for two with meals included ($215-$250 off-season). Tel: 284-495-8002. Fax: 284-495-9362. www.anegadareef.com*

SNORKELING

The waters around the BVI look incredibly peaceful. But stick your head below the surface and you'll see that there's an amazing amount of stuff going on down there.

Even if you don't really like to swim, consider snorkeling in the BVI at least once. The water is astonishingly clear, there are great shipwrecks to explore, and the millions of brightly-colored fish are amazing to see.

Trying to point out the best snorkeling places in the BVI would be sort of like trying to list good French restaurants in Paris. The waters around the British Virgin Islands are teeming with fish — everywhere, right up to the very shoreline.

In fact, if you stand anywhere along the water's edge and drop in broken up bits of stale rolls, it will only be a minute or two before fish will show up to eat. Sometimes the fish will nibble right out of your hand!

How to Snorkel
Snorkeling is something even the most timid soul can try. You can just wade in from the beach with a snorkel and mask and stick your head underwater. Most beaches have excellent snorkeling areas at one or both ends, or wherever a reef has grown. You can also go on organized snorkeling trips all over

IN THE BVI

the BVI. The truly decadent snorkelers simply lie down on one of those brightly-colored yellow floats and stick their head over the edge!

Snorkeling Over Sand
You can snorkel almost anywhere, and beginners are sometimes most comfortable just wading into calm water from the beach and snorkeling over the sand. You'll get to see some fish and you can look for rays, which are the color of the sand and almost impossible to see unless they decide to move. You can also look for turtles and sand dollars.

Snorkeling Over Reefs
The most colorful sea creatures cluster around reefs. It's here that you will see fish, some much smaller than an inch, in all manner of gaudy costumes: bold white and orange stripes, bright purple speckled with silver stars, iridescent stripes of blue and chartreuse. But it's not just the reef fish that are colorful. So is the reef. Watch for the many types of coral. Look for sponges and sea anemones and starfish. And look around you in the water. A great sight to catch is a family of baby squid, each less than half an inch in length, hanging still in a perfect row.

Great Reefs and Great Snorkeling Trips
You can find colorful reefs just offshore of virtually every BVI beach. Or you can take a boat trip to a great snorkeling spot (see pages 70, 102, and 110).

SNORKELING HINTS

❏When you are snorkeling, never ever touch anything. Sea urchins (those round, black things with thin, black spikes sticking up) and certain corals can sting badly.

❏Also, never ever stand on anything but sand. Coral reefs are exceptionally fragile and grow incredibly slowly. What you destroy with a single crunch of your flipper will take years to replace.

❏To really see what is going on around a reef, try to hover and stare at one particular section. At first you may notice just a few things. But keep looking. The longer you look at one spot, the more activity you'll see.

❏If your mask keeps fogging up, rinse it in the sea water, spit onto the inside, rub the spit all around the glass, rinse the mask briefly, and put it back on. Or buy a defogger (but the spit works equally well and you are less likely to run out).

❏If you forgot your prescription mask (or didn't even know you could get one), you can buy them in the BVI at almost any dive shop.

4. COOPER

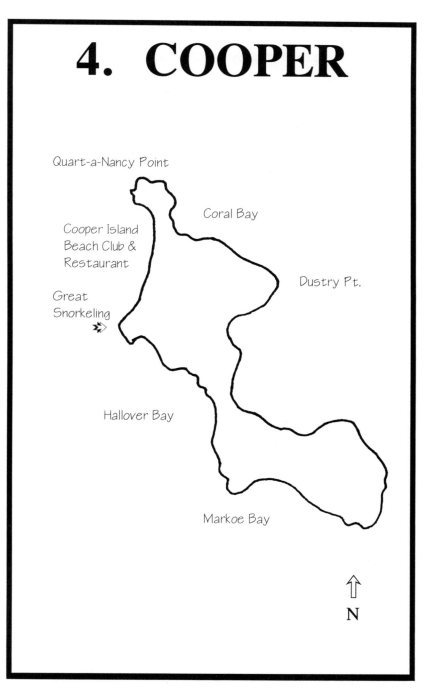

Quart-a-Nancy Point

Coral Bay

Cooper Island
Beach Club &
Restaurant

Dustry Pt.

Great
Snorkeling

Hallover Bay

Markoe Bay

↑
N

COOPER

Cooper Island is a small but hilly island that has long been popular with the charter boat crowd. There's a little beach and some outstanding snorkeling. There's also a casual restaurant, a nice little barefoot bar, a boutique, a dive shop, a couple of houses, and a little resort. And that's it! There are no roads on this island and only about six people live here.

This spot is a great get-away. And even though it's isolated if you stay here, every night you can meet a new group of people at the bar who have anchored for the night. It's kind of fun to be a "local" and watch people come and go. If you want to visit Tortola, hop on the ferry Monday, Wednesday, or Friday. Each week during the season there is a scheduled trip to Peter Island and also to Virgin Gorda.

If you want to come here just for the day, you can come by ferry from Prospect Reef (see Appendix) or rent a boat or take a boat trip here (see pages 70, 102, 110). Also check local papers for special events here.

Cooper Island Restaurant (VHF Channel 16) has been here for years. It's a little open-air place which looks out over the bay. For lunch you can get hamburgers, conch fritters, catch of the day, and superb ratatouille. Luckily, you can also get the ratatouille for dinner as an appetizer. Dinner specialties include veal marsala, grilled steak, and beef curry. The bar is truly barefoot, and it's open all day.

The **Cooper Island Beach Club** is a modest but appealing group of 12 comfortable rooms (two to a building) set among palm trees just 50 feet from the beach and furnished in rattan, each with books and games and a kitchenette. Bring your groceries from Road Town or give them a list in advance. *12 rooms. General Manager: Chris Tillings. Rates: $175 per night for two people ($115 spring and fall; $95 summer). Reservations: 800-542-4624. Tel: 284-494-3721. E-mail: info@cooper-island.com.*

"Life is too short for traffic."

— *Unknown*

HELPFUL HINTS

❑On the BVI, as on many islands, people exchange greetings and inquire about each other's health before getting down to business. This is true whether they run into a friend, stop for gas, go to the grocery store, or order food from a waitress. It's considered very rude to skip this conversational step.

❑In these islands, when you didn't hear what someone said, the polite way to ask for a repeat is to say "Say again?" or "Please repeat" rather than "What?"

❑It may puzzle you that sometimes you can't always understand the British Virgin Islanders even though they are speaking English. This is not just because of the West Indian accent. It is also because the idioms are different. In the states, you "go for a swim," didn't "hear" something, "turn" a latch, say "Yes." Islanders "take a sea bath," didn't "catch" something, "swing" a latch, and say "It would seem so." A list of all the idiomatic differences would fill a book.

❑Most islanders are actually going out of their way to talk "your language" when they talk to you. They are speaking extra slowly and avoiding the local phrases that seem to most confuse visitors. (Try listening to a group of islanders chatting among themselves and you'll see how much faster and more idiomatically they talk.)

THINGS PEOPLE USUALLY WISH THEY HAD KNOWN SOONER

❑**Bugs.** Keep a little container of bug repellant (like a Cutter stick) with you *at all times*. This is actually a good idea if you are traveling anywhere in the Caribbean. It's not that any place is always buggy, it just can be buggy practically anywhere when there is absolutely no breeze.

❑**Itchy bug bites.** If you get bitten and have nothing to stop the itch, remember that a dab of straight gin or vodka usually works (you're supposed to apply it directly to the bite, but some people swear it works just as well if you drink it instead).

❑**Soap but no water.** When you are in a washroom in the BVI (or, in fact, almost anywhere in the Caribbean), check that water will actually come out of the faucet before you put that liquid soap on your hands. It's tough to get it all off if there's no water around. (It can be handy to carry wash & dries with you.)

❑**Missing meals.** If you are flying from the states to the BVI via Puerto Rico, you will discover that connections often make it impossible to eat for many hours, so tuck some food and a bottle of water in your carry-on.

❑**Holidays.** On major public holidays (see Appendix), almost everything in the BVI closes up.

❑**ATM machines.** Most BVI banks have them but they rarely work, so don't count on getting cash this way.

5. GUANA

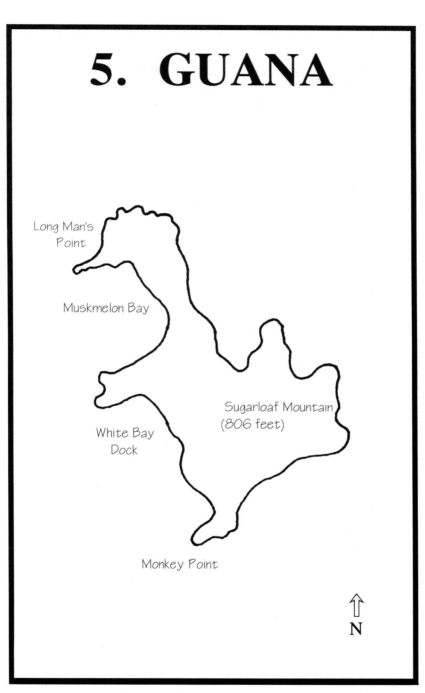

Long Man's Point

Muskmelon Bay

White Bay Dock

Sugarloaf Mountain (806 feet)

Monkey Point

N

GUANA

*Guana, at 850 acres, is the seventh largest British Virgin Island. It is extremely hilly and very private and home to the wonderful **Guana Island** resort. All of the island is a nature preserve and wildlife and bird sanctuary and there are rare roseate flamingos, masked boobys, and frigate birds, and many kinds of herons. At least 50 species of birds are regularly found there. Scientists from several academic institutions are engaged in on-going studies of Guana Island's flora and fauna.*

Peaceful walks meander through lush tropical greenery and brilliant flowering bushes and trees. There are seven usually empty beaches and lots of hiking trails that go all over the island. Staying here is a one-of-a-kind experience. It is simple, very civilized, and incredibly relaxing. The island is truly private. The dining room is not open to outside guests and there are no day trippers on the island.

The **Guana Island** resort is perched on the top of one of Guana Island's hills and there are astonishingly beautiful panoramic views in every direction. Appealing rooms, most in cottages with handsome stone walls and beamed ceilings, are simply decorated but very comfortable. Many have separate sitting areas and all have large porches or balconies and very private entrances. Breakfast, lunch, and dinner are served on a stone terrace and guests gather in the drawing room for before-dinner cocktails and after-dinner cognacs. Dinner is a casually elegant affair with several courses and guests can dine with other guests or at private tables, whichever they prefer. Most guests do some of each.

There are seven beautiful and usually deserted beaches, a little honor beach bar, good snorkeling spots, tennis courts, and various water activities are available. Hiking trails lead to beaches and secluded vistas. You can spend days hiking and swimming or reclined on the beach or your private terrace absorbed in a book or just taking in the views. This is a remarkably relaxing spot to visit. *15 units. General Managers: Birget Bihler and Mark Ferris. Rates, which include meals, house wines with lunch and dinner, and use of all equipment: $850 in season for a double ($650 off-season). Rent-the-Island rates are $15,000 per day ($11,500 off-season). Reservations: 800-544-8262. Tel: 914-967-6050. Fax: 914-967-8048. Local Tel: 284-494-2354. www. guana.com.*

DID YOU KNOW?

❏If you pushed all the British Virgin Islands together into one land mass, it would only cover 59 square miles. That's about the same size as Nantucket Island. Or one twentieth the size of Rhode Island, the smallest state in the union.

❏William Thornton, who designed the U.S. Capitol building, was born in the BVI in 1759 on the island of Jost Van Dyke.

❏Only about 18,000 people live in the BVI. Seven times this number of people live in Stamford, Connecticut. And twice this many people live in Beverly Hills, California. If everybody in the entire BVI took a seat in the 80,000-seat New Orleans Superdome, there would still be 52,000 empty seats!

❏Latitudinally, the BVI are located roughly half-way between the equator and New York City.

❏It's only about ten degrees warmer in the summer than in the winter in the BVI. Winter temperatures average about 75 degrees, summer about 85 degrees.

❏If you headed directly east from the BVI, you would eventually be in the Sahara Desert. As a matter of fact, in the BVI in the summer the air is sometimes hazy because it is full of Sahara dust, fine particles of sand that have been blown by the Trade Winds all the way from Africa. You can actually feel a fine grittiness on the surface of things.

❑The wind in the BVI generally blows in the opposite direction from the winds that sweep across the United States and Europe. On these continents, the wind and the weather generally come from the west. In the BVI, the winds and the weather generally come out of the east.

❑The BVI really does have seasons. Although it rarely ever rains for long, in the winter there are more frequent two-minute cloudbursts (which keep the hills emerald green), the humidity is low, and there are very steady Trade Winds. Summer is frequently dry (the hills can turn brown), more humid, and less windy.

❑The Christmas winds, which usually start (you guessed it) just around Christmas, are strong and sometimes stay at 30 to 40 knots for several days.

❑The flat road on Tortola that runs between Road Town and West End wasn't built until 1966 when they reclaimed that flat land from the sea. As recently as 1965 it was an all-day trip by donkey from that end of the island to town! You'll still catch sight of old-timers traveling the old-fashioned way!

6. JOST VAN DYKE

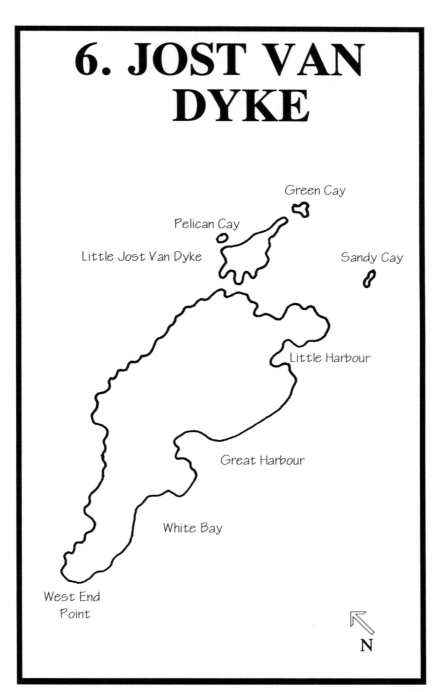

Green Cay

Pelican Cay

Little Jost Van Dyke

Sandy Cay

Little Harbour

Great Harbour

White Bay

West End
Point

N

JOST VAN DYKE IN A NUTSHELL

Jost Van Dyke is four miles long, hilly, and home to just 163 people. It has a tiny resort, great beach restaurants and bars, and is known by yachters around the world for its gentle anchorages and for Foxy and his famous Tamarind Bar, one of the most celebrated bars in the entire Caribbean.

There are three areas to visit: Great Harbour, Little Harbour, and White Bay. Restaurants are casual, open-air, and waterfront. It's very quiet here off-season and places can be closed much of September. For places to stay on Jost Van Dyke, see page 40.

WHAT YOU CAN DO ON JOST VAN DYKE

This is an excellent one-day adventure. It's a half-hour ferry ride from Tortola. You can walk along the beach, swim, snorkel, hike, eat good food, and visit bars in a delightfully relaxed, "no-shoes required" atmosphere. You can catch a ferry in the late afternoon or you can also stay for dinner and head home after dark— a nighttime boat ride under a sky full of brilliant stars with the lights of Tortola twinkling in the distance is hard to beat!

THE FERRY RIDE FROM TORTOLA

What to bring on a day trip: *some cash (not every place takes credit cards), swimsuit, towel, sunscreen, camera, film, snorkel equipment. Bare feet are the norm at restaurants, but bring sturdy shoes if you want to hike the hills or walk the road.*

CATCHING THE FERRY

In the BVI, the ferry to Jost Van Dyke leaves from West End, Tortola (see Appendix for Ferry Schedules). It's generally a steel-hulled boat named *When*, so named, many say, because the *When* leaves whenever it's ready. It's really a delivery boat for goods rather than people, and once it's loaded, it leaves. Departure might be a half hour late, but it can also be fifteen minutes early! Get to the dock with time to spare. Locate the ferry (it should be at the left end of the dock as you walk through the dock's entryway). If it's still being loaded, you probably have time to pick up a soda across the street at Zelma's or a beer to go at the Harbour View Restaurant. Then go sit somewhere close to the *When* and enjoy the sights of the harbor. Those pastel buildings across the water are Pusser's Landing, a Pusser's Store, and shops.

Generally, the only indication that the boat is actually leaving is when someone begins to untie the lines. This is your cue to hop aboard. By the way, sometimes you buy a ticket before boarding and sometimes you pay the $10 fare when you get to Jost Van Dyke and sometimes the *Nubian Princess* is the boat instead of the *When*, so ask someone when you get there. Also, the *Paradise Express* sometimes runs, too.

GREAT SIGHTS TO LOOK FOR FROM THE FERRY
As you leave the dock, watch for the interesting-looking grey house built right into a cliff on the right, on Tortola's point, and the picturesque island across the water on your left. For years the rumor was that the guy who built the grey house also bought this island, which is known as Little Thatch, so he could look across at an unspoiled view! However, Little Thatch is now an exclusive resort (see page 48).

Once the boat turns right and you clear passage between Great Thatch (on the left) and Tortola, Jost Van Dyke will be dead ahead and Tortola's north shore will appear on the right. Those two big green "gum drops" of land on Tortola define Smuggler's Cove. Just beyond the further "gum drop" is Long Bay. You can't see Cane Garden Bay, but the distant hill with a long scar of erosion is at its far edge.

Approaching Jost Van Dyke, you'll see two tiny islands on the right, each with a brilliant strip of white sand. The one closest to Jost Van Dyke is Green Cay. The other is Sandy Cay and is owned by Laurance Rockefeller. You can also see a strip of road that runs along Jost's hillside. This is the only road on the island.

ARRIVING AT GREAT HARBOUR
The ferry takes you to the public dock in Great Harbour, the main "town" on Jost Van Dyke. White Bay and Little Harbour can be reached by land or water taxi.

GREAT HARBOUR

Great Harbour is simply a strip of beach with some casual bars and restaurants and a couple of little stores scattered along the shore. The public dock leads right to the little two-story Customs House. You don't need to stop here unless you happen to be coming from the USVI.

The water here is good for swimming and snorkeling, but watch out for dinghies speeding about. By the way, when you are on the beach at Great Harbour looking out across the water, virtually all the distant hills you see are part of St. John (USVI).

GREAT HARBOUR'S GREAT RESTAURANTS AND BARS

Note: Even though Jost Van Dyke is extremely casual, you should make dinner reservations by late afternoon because supplies on the island are quite limited. (If they know you are coming, they'll speed off to another island and get food if necessary.)

Foxy's Tamarind Bar (495-9258) serves great food (some of the very best on the island) and gallons of their irresistible Painkiller Punch, but the real draw here is Foxy himself, who is never without his guitar. He sings during lunch and cocktail hour every day but Sunday, but also wanders in and out all day long, happy to create impromptu, amusing ballads about his guests. Come here for burgers, flying fish sandwiches, and rotis for lunch, and grilled fresh fish, steak, and lobster for dinner. Friday and Saturday there's a barbecue. Despite the immense popularity of this place, and the occasional crowds, the atmosphere here remains remarkably casual, unhurried, and pleasant thanks to Foxy's wife, Tessa, and to Gary and his exceptionally professional staff. *Restaurant closed late August through September but bar often stays open and you might find Foxy.*

Club Paradise (495-9267) serves good black bean soup, cheeseburgers, and West Indian specialties like conch stew for lunch, and fresh fish and steak for dinner. There's a pig roast Wednesday nights. Dinner can seem a bit hectic, but the staff manages well and keeps on smiling. Happy Hour is 4 to 5 pm in the little bar when all drinks are two-for-one.

Happy Laury's Snack Bar (495-9259) is the spot for honey-dipped chicken, cheeseburgers, and cold sodas and beer.

Ali Baba's (495-9280) serves hamburgers, conch fritters, and rotis and has an inviting bar. Don't miss the Monday evening all-you-can-eat pig roast.

Christine's Bakery (495-9281) is THE place to come for breakfast. Sit outside on the terrace and order anything from eggs and bacon to fresh fruit to freshly-baked coconut bread, doughnuts, or Christine's exceptional cinnamon and raisin sweet rolls. (It's been said that as long as you consume these delicious rolls before noon they have nary a calorie!) At lunch, Christine serves chicken rotis, flying fish sandwiches, burgers, and fish with West Indian sauce. Dinner specialties include fish, chicken, and stewed conch.

GREAT HARBOUR NIGHTLIFE

Foxy's Tamarind Bar. Foxy, himself, entertains during lunch and cocktail hour every day but Sunday. On Thursday and Saturday nights "Focus" headlines, playing everything from soft rock to calypso. Friday nights "O-2" pumps out reggae and rock selections. Sunday afternoons a band plays calypso and light jazz. Most other evenings a DJ takes over.

Club Paradise. A steel band usually plays Wednesday evenings.

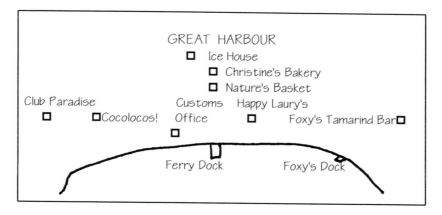

"It was supposed to be open for only one day, for the Harvest Festival in 1967."

— Foxy Callwood,
smiling as he commented on his famous Tamarind Bar,
which he has now kept open for more than 30 years!

SHOPPING AT GREAT HARBOUR

Cocolocos!!! sells delightfully colorful, one-of-a-kind, handmade t-shirts. There are also interesting jumpsuits, skirts, and tops for women, plus a "kid's corner" with mini-size hats, t-shirts, and jump-suits, and a great selection of hats for all ages. In contrast to the U.S., an appealing sign urges you to unfold and look at as many t-shirts as you wish (because they are all different) and another sign describing hours of operation begins like this: "Hours inconsistent. Sometimes we're open in the morning...."

Foxy's Boutique is the place to come for soft cotton dresses, casual resortwear, colorful t-shirts and swimwear and shorts for the whole family, cassette tapes and CDs of island music (including Foxy's, naturally), books, postcards, sunscreen, batteries, a variety of unusual gift items, and more.

Nature's Basket features exquisite fruits grown up in the hills on Jost Van Dyke. Come here for deliciously sweet pineapples, papayas, mangoes, and bananas. You'll also find fresh vegetables, cheeses, canned goods, and sodas.

Christine's Bakery showcases delicious breads and rolls including coconut and banana bread and brownies, cakes, pies, and doughnuts — all freshly baked, plus, of course, her irresistible cinnamon and raisin sweet rolls.

Rudy's Suprette, at the opposite end of the beach from Foxy's, carries canned goods, bottled water, sodas, crackers, beer, and a variety of miscellaneous items which change depending on what the supply boat delivers. If you are looking for almost anything, there's a chance you'll find it here.

The Ice House, which is at the end of the little road past Christine's, is the place to go for ice — by the cube and by the block.

GREAT NATURE WALKS

Ivan Chinnery (495-9312) will take you on really wonderful nature walks on Jost Van Dyke. One of the best routes is up in the hills above Great Harbour where he grows his own pineapples, mangoes, papayas, and bananas. He'll cut a branch of bananas for you — when they're still green and hard. Follow Ivan's advice and keep the bananas until they turn yellow. Then wait yet one more day before you bite into one. The fruit will be incredibly sweet and delicious. His pineapples are also exceptional. You can buy all of Ivan's produce at Nature's Basket in Great Harbour.

LITTLE HARBOUR

Little Harbour is a popular anchorage but there is virtually no beach. There are several casual restaurants at the water's edge.

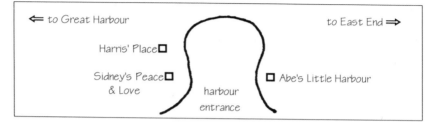

GETTING THERE

You can go from the Great Harbour dock to Little Harbour by water via **Gregory's Brat Water Taxi** in about five minutes for $5 per person. He also rents little power boats (if you can't find him, ask around). Vancito George (495-9253) drives a land taxi and fares between Great Harbour and Little Harbour run about $5 per person. Look for his taxi around the Customs Building. Ali Baba, Gerald Chinnery, and Abe Cockle also drive taxis.

RESTAURANTS AND BARS

Harris' Place (495-9302) cooks up breakfast, hamburgers and sandwiches for lunch, and West Indian fish and lobster for dinner. On Monday nights there is a lobster cookout.

Sidney's Peace & Love (495-9271) prepares breakfast plus lobster, chicken, fish, and West Indian dishes for lunch and dinner.

Abe's Little Harbour (VHF Channel 16) serves lobster, chicken, fish, conch, and spare ribs for lunch and dinner and holds a pig roast every Wednesday night. They also have a pool table.

ENTERTAINMENT

Sidney's Peace & Love. One of Tortola's most popular bands, "O-2," performs here several nights a week.

Harris' Place. Ruben Chinnery plays guitar and sings ballads and more Monday nights.

WHITE BAY

White Bay has a long and lovely beach, interrupted midway by an outcropping of rock. On the far side of the rocks from Great Harbour is a small resort and restaurant and a lively bar that is a popular lunch stop. At the near end of the beach, just over the hill from Great Harbour, is a little restaurant and a campground with cabins.

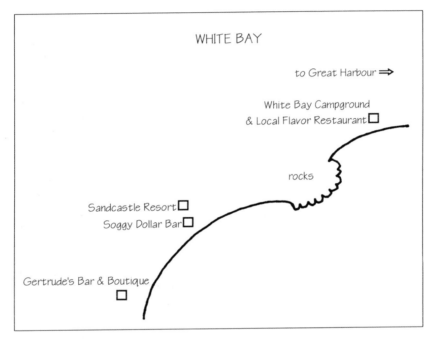

WHITE BAY

to Great Harbour ⟹

White Bay Campground
& Local Flavor Restaurant ☐

rocks

Sandcastle Resort ☐
Soggy Dollar Bar ☐

Gertrude's Bar & Boutique
☐

GETTING THERE

The quickest and most enjoyable way is the five-minute water taxi ride from the Great Harbour dock. **Gregory's Brat Water Taxi** speeds you over in a little Boston Whaler-type boat and the fare is $5 per person. Look for the water taxi on the dock or ask at Cocolocos! (her husband runs the water taxi). You can also rent a dinghy from Greg.

You can walk to White Bay. It's a good 20 minute walk over a very tough hill (okay in the morning but a killer in the afternoon sun) to the very beginning of the beach, and another 15 minutes to get to the far end of the beach and Sandcastle. You can also take a land taxi.

RESTAURANTS AND BARS

Soggy Dollar Bar (495-9888) at the Sandcastle Resort claims to be the originator of rum painkillers (according to a letter on the wall) and this smooth blend is the house specialty. Lunch is casual but delicious. Choose from excellent hamburgers, great jerk chicken or flying fish sandwiches, and try some excellent conch fritters. Order lunch at the bar and then carry it to a table or to the beach. After lunch you can rest in one of several hammocks slung between the trees. Dinner is far more elegant, and is served by candlelight in the charming dining room around the corner from the bar. The four-course menu changes but choice of appetizers might include West Indian pumpkin or black bean soup and main courses might be sauteed mahi with ginger and lime sauce, pork tenderloin with spicy plum puree, or grilled salmon with a citrus marinade. The dessert list usually includes key lime pie and rum bananas. This is also a great place to come for breakfast, which is served until 11 am. Try the banana pancakes or delicious French toast. *Usually closed mid-September to mid-October. Breakfast $10, lunch around $10, dinner $30. Reservations essential by 4 pm for dinner.*

Gertrude's Beach Bar and Boutique is usually set up on a table a bit further along the beach. It's a quite informal spot to get a drink or buy a t-shirt.

The Local Flavor Restaurant (495-9312) is open for breakfast, lunch, and Saturday night barbecues. It's a small spot at the east end of White Bay, just over the hill from Great Harbour. Here you can get hamburgers, flying fish sandwiches, and West Indian-style dishes. Bring an instrument on Saturday night and join the festive jam session. *Closed off-season.*

Entertainment on White Bay

Soggy Dollar Bar. Ruben Chinnery strums the guitar and sings ballads and soft rock every Sunday afternoon.

RUBEN CHINNERY AND HIS GUITAR

Don't miss Ruben Chinnery. He plays guitar and brings the "Ruben" touch to popular songs and well-known ballads. He seems to travel effortlessly, showing up on island after island, sharing his beautiful music almost everywhere. Check the *Limin Times* to see where you can catch him next. If you see him scheduled on two different islands on the same day, it's probably not a mistake!

JOST VAN DYKE RESORTS AND GUEST HOUSES

There are very few facilities for staying overnight on Jost Van Dyke. Most people who come here arrive on their own boat or on a charter boat and spend the night anchored or moored off-shore.

GREAT HARBOUR

Paradise Guest House offers simple rooms which can hit the spot when you just have to get off the boat and spend a night on land or if you want to spend a night right on Great Harbour. They're above Christine's Bakery. *4 rooms. Shared bath, no a/c. $85 on-season, $65 off-season for two people. Tel: 284-495-9281. Fax: 284-495-9892.*

WHITE BAY

Sandcastle, on White Bay, is a delightful, tiny hideaway. Four hexagonal, simply furnished but quite charming cottages are set in the trees at the edge of lovely White Bay beach and ceiling fans capture the sea breezes. There are also two additional more traditionally-shaped rooms. This is the place to come when you want to read, relax, lie in a hammock, make forays to other beaches, and come back for a quiet candlelit dinner. If you want, you can always take a ferry to Tortola for the day. The restaurant is excellent. *6 units. Rates: $220 ($150 off-season) for two people not including taxes or meals. Owners/ Managers: Debby Pearse and Bruce Donath. Tel: 284-495-9888. Fax: 284-495-9999. Usually closed mid-September through mid-October.*

White Bay Campgrounds and Cabins are run by Ivan Chinnery. There are four equipped campsites (lamp and bed and ice chest inside a tent) for $35 a night; ten bare campsites for $15 a night; and eight screened cabins with lamp, bed, and ice chest for $40 to $55 a night. Bathrooms and showers are near. *Tel: 284-495-9312.*

JOST VAN DYKE'S EAST END

Sandy Ground Estates is on East End, over a big hill from Little Harbour, and isolated. These one-, two-, and three-bedroom houses are above a beach. Guests bring provisions or management will stock the house. The nearest restaurant is a long (and hilly) walk away. *8 villas. Rates: $1400 a week for two people ($980 off-season). Tel: 284-494-3391. Fax: 284-495-9379.*

WONDERFUL SIGHTS TO LOOK FOR

Goats in boats. If you think you've lost your mind because you think you see a dinghy full of animals out there, keep looking. It's probably goats. Islanders keep their goats on many of the uninhabited islands, and move them around on occasion, and it is not unusual to catch sight of a Boston Whaler with ten or twelve goats milling around!

Sea turtles. When you are snorkeling or floating or boating, look for big sea turtles. Before a turtle surfaces, it surreptitiously sticks its head out of the water to see what is going on. You can easily mistake it for a drifting stick.

Rays. You can sometimes spot a ray at rest when you are snorkeling over sand. Study the bottom carefully. They lie perfectly still and are almost indistinguishable from the sand.

Rainbows. Brilliant rainbows show up everywhere in the BVI, all day long. Even the briefest rain somewhere in the distance can create a rainbow and you'll get to see it splashed across the sky, radiant in the sunlight.

Double rainbows. The very luckiest people get to see complete double rainbows. Even a partial double is good luck.

Shooting stars. Just stare at the night sky for a few minutes and you're bound to catch a shooting star or a satellite streaking through the brilliant nighttime canopy. Some shooting stars are high in the sky but others are so big and fall so close they'll take your breath away.

Hummingbirds. They hang fluttering in the air close to flowering bushes, in glistening greens and blues.

41

FERRYING AROUND THE BVI

Ferries are an extremely pleasant way to travel around the BVI or to visit St. John or St. Thomas in the USVI. Many ferries have at least some open-air seating. Usually you can sit outside and watch the scenery. You'll get a lot of sun here, but the air is nice and the views are just wonderful. (And it can be a bit close down below.) Even if a brief shower comes by, you'll be dry before you reach your destination. Do check the seas. If they are rough, it can be splashy on the windward side so try to sit on the leeward side.

Ferries run between Tortola and Jost Van Dyke, Virgin Gorda (North Sound and the Valley), Cooper Island, Peter Island, and Marina Cay, and St. Thomas and St. John in the U.S. Virgin Islands. Ferries also run between Jost Van Dyke and St. Thomas and St. John on weekends.

Two ferry lines run between both Tortola and the Valley on Virgin Gorda and Tortola and St. Thomas. When you arrive at the dock, representatives from each company may try to convince you to take their ferry. Although the people are well-meaning, it can be annoying and confusing when you are trying to pay the cab driver and don't know which ferry you want. If you haven't already decided what ferry to take, just say so firmly and you will be left alone.

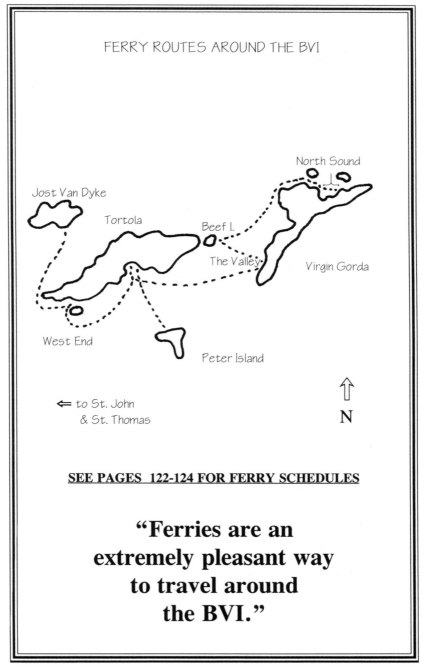

FERRY ROUTES AROUND THE BVI

North Sound

Jost Van Dyke

Tortola

Beef I.

The Valley

Virgin Gorda

West End

Peter Island

⟸ to St. John
& St. Thomas

⇑
N

SEE PAGES 122-124 FOR FERRY SCHEDULES

"Ferries are an extremely pleasant way to travel around the BVI."

AMAZING NIGHTS
IN THE BVI

★ Anchoring in Cane Garden Bay and hearing
the melodic sounds of local recording star
Quito Rhymer
drift across the water — beautiful ballads
and love songs accompanied by sweet guitar

★ Any beach on a moonless night,
when the sky is ablaze with about ten times more stars
than you have ever before seen

★ Bomba's Full-Moon Parties on Tortola,
when there seem to be more people
than you thought lived in the entire BVI

★ Foxy's much-loved and very famous
New Year's Eve extravaganzas
on Jost Van Dyke — when there are
so many boats at anchor
that you can practically hop
from boat to boat all the way to the shore

★ Dancing cheek-to-cheek under the stars
at elegant Biras Creek or Little Dix Bay

★ Walking a deserted beach
under a brilliant full moon,
when it's so bright that the possibility of "moon-burn"
occurs to you for the very first time

7. MARINA CAY

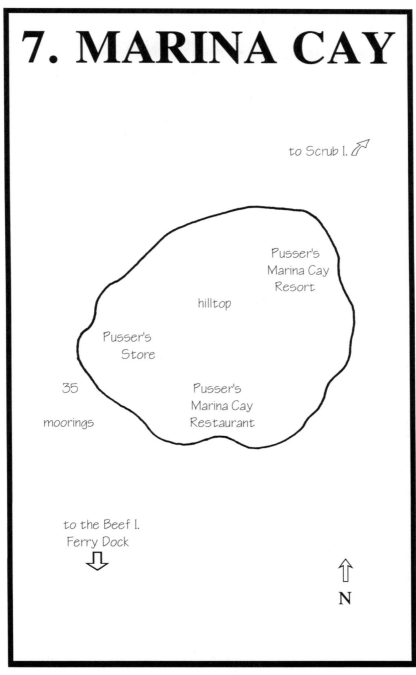

to Scrub I.

Pusser's
Marina Cay
Resort

hilltop

Pusser's
Store

35

Pusser's
Marina Cay
Restaurant

moorings

to the Beef I.
Ferry Dock

N

MARINA CAY

This tiny bit of rock that pokes its head out of the water between Beef Island and Great Camanoe is hardly big enough to be called an island. Indeed, it covers just eight acres! It's a great anchorage and there are 35 moorings here and it's the site of the Pusser's Marina Cay Resort, Pusser's Marina Cay Restaurant, and a Pusser's Company Store.

WHAT YOU CAN DO ON MARINA CAY

You can dine or have a drink at the restaurant and shop in Pusser's. You can also sun yourself on the little beach, swim in calm water, and enjoy great snorkeling over the shallow reef that extends out from much of this islet. It's possible to walk completely around Marina Cay in a very short amount of time provided you have shoes to protect your feet from the rocks and the sharp coral.

HOW TO GET THERE

There are free ferries from Beef Island at the ferry dock right next to the Conch Shell Point Restaurant. See page 124 for schedules.

Pusser's Marina Cay Restaurant (494-2174) sits along the edge of the beach and is open for lunch and dinner. Appetizers include conch fritters and Caribbean nachos. At lunch you can get hot dogs, burgers, burritos, and various salads. The dinner menu includes ribs, steak, lobster, fish, and pasta.

Pusser's Company Store (494-2174) is built out over the water and features the Pusser's line of wearable clothing for the whole family, plus books, nautical memorabilia, swimwear, post cards, and much more.

Pusser's Marina Cay Resort units are on the opposite side of the hillside from the restaurant and look out over the water. Four rooms each have a king size bed, a little refrigerator, ceiling fans (no air conditioning, but it's almost always very breezy here), and balcony. There are also two two-bedroom suites. Continental breakfast is included in the rates. Guests can rent hobie cats or ocean kayaks or head across to Trellis Bay to windsurf. And, of course, they can take the ferry to Beef Island and explore Tortola for the day. *6 units. Rates: $175 a night for two ($120 off-season); suites $450 ($295 off-season). General Managers: Roger and Sandy Garside. Tel: 284-494-2174. Fax: 284-494-4775. P.O. Box 626. E-mail: marinacay@pussers.com.*

8. NECKER

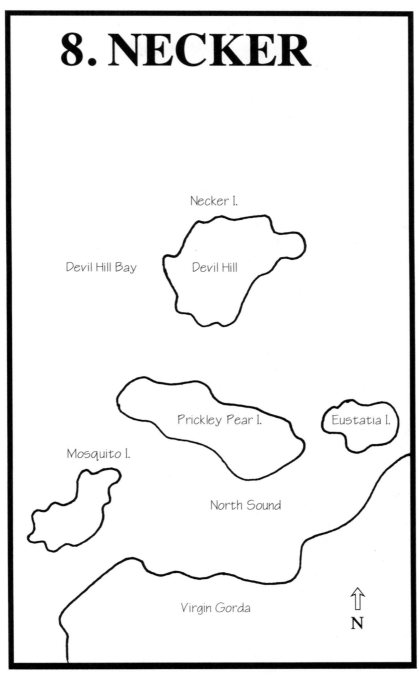

Necker I.

Devil Hill Bay   Devil Hill

Prickley Pear I.   Eustatia I.

Mosquito I.

North Sound

Virgin Gorda

↑
N

NECKER

Necker is a luxurious, 74-acre private island surrounded by coral reefs that sits just north of Virgin Gorda and you rent the whole thing. This is the place to come if you want a lot of privacy and plenty of pampering. Mel Gibson, Harrison Ford, Oprah Winfrey, and Steven Spielberg are just some of the many famous guests who have rented here. You can swim at empty beaches, dine on gourmet food, and walk along winding paths through brilliant tropical flowers. At stops on every walk are baskets full of sodas, wine, and cold champagne, just in case that's what you were thinking of having.

Two times a year one can make room reservations at Necker. During these Celebration Weeks, up to 13 couples arrive to a kind of "house-party" setting, sharing the living quarters and dining together.

Necker Island is a truly luxurious tropical paradise. White sand beaches ring the shoreline and brilliant tropical flowers seem to be everywhere. Perched on a hill is a Balinese villa with a sort of giant, high-ceilinged, indoor-outdoor living room open to soft breezes. Bedroom doors fold back completely, providing awesome views right from your pillow. Resident chefs work magic in the state-of-the-art kitchen and a staff of 24 await your requests. Paths lead through the manicured grounds to beaches, swimming pools, tennis court, a 300-year old Hindu meditation hut, and hidden hammocks. *General Managers: Mark and Joanne Netherwood. Rates: $14,000 a day 1-7 people, $18,500 a day 8-14 people, $24,000 a day 15-19 people, $29,000 a day 20-26 people. Celebration Weeks: $13,000 per couple for the week. Rates include almost everything. Reservations: 800-557-4255.*

LITTLE THATCH

If you want something a bit smaller than Necker, head to this glorious hilltop retreat on a 55-acre island just west of Tortola. Views from the open-air main house and the private terraces of the five bedrooms showcase stunning views of nearby islands. In between fine cuisine, float in the "disappearing edge" pool or wander down to the picture-perfect beach or lie in a hammock and watch the stars. *General Manager: Jon Morley. Rates: $10,450 per day, 1-4 people, $11,755 per day 5-10 people. Tel: 284-495-9227. Fax: 284-495-9212. E-mail: thatch@caribsurf.com. Closed August-October.*

RAINY DAYS

Rainy days are rare in the British Virgin Islands but if it happens to rain on one of the days you are in the BVI, here are some great things to do.

❖ Schedule a massage or a yoga class
at Ft. Recovery.

❖ Find someone you love and take a
long rainy walk on the beach.

❖ Get a book and read quietly where you can
see and hear the rain and
smell the tropical moisture
but still keep dry
(in light rains a palm tree is fine shelter).

❖ Write and send a dozen postcards to people
you like, or to people you don't like.

❖ Go for a swim in a pool.

❖ Play a board game, like Parcheesi or Clue.
Most places have these games around
and they're still fun, whether you are 12 or 112.
Or buy one at the **Learn & Fun Shop**
in Road Town.

❖ Take photographs — rain showers, rainbows,
slick palm fronds, patterns of rain on water.

SCUBA DIVING

Many people have no idea that dive outfits in the BVI offer simple Resort Courses where qualified instructors teach you how to dive in just a few hours, in the safety of a quiet pool, and then take you out for a real dive over a reef or a wreck. You go down 40 to 50 feet with trained instructors by your side.

Many who have tried this go on to become certified divers. Almost everybody says that it is an amazing and wonderful experience, and some say it is even easier than snorkeling.

For experienced divers, the BVI offer some exceptionally interesting shipwrecks, including the 2,434 ton *H.M.S. Rhone*, plus caves, reefs, walls, pinnacles, ledges, and archways, all in unusually clear water. Night dives, which show off amazing things you can't see during the day, are popular here, too.

*On Tortola, call **Baskin' in the Sun** at Prospect Reef in Road Town (494-2858) or Soper's Hole (495-4582) or **Underwater Safaris** at The Moorings in Road Town (494-3235) and also at Cooper Island.*

*On Virgin Gorda **DIVE BVI** works out of Leverick Bay (495-7328) and the Virgin Gorda Yacht Harbour (495-5513) and also at Marina Cay and Peter Island. **Kilbride's Underwater Tours** is at the Bitter End Yacht Club on Virgin Gorda's North Sound (495-9638).*

9.PETER

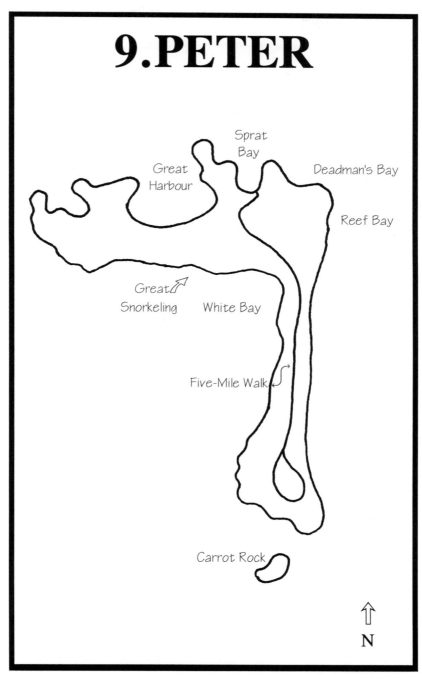

Sprat Bay

Great Harbour

Deadman's Bay

Reef Bay

Great Snorkeling

White Bay

Five-Mile Walk

Carrot Rock

N

PETER

Peter Island is a lush and mountainous private island five miles south of Tortola. The Peter Island Resort and Yacht Harbour is nestled along the north shore and there are five beautiful beaches. What magazine articles and books omit about this fine resort is that the resort facilities only take up a tiny bit of this four and a half mile long island. The rest of the island is undeveloped, except for the Eagle's Nest, a private residence that sits atop the island's highest point. Although there are no cars on the island, several roads lead through this hilly woodland and there are marvelous opportunities for long, scenic walks, including the famous five-mile walk that starts from Sprat Bay. Several bays on Peter Island are popular anchorages and there are moorings on Sprat Bay. The ferry schedule (see page 124) makes it easy to come from Road Town for the whole day or just for dinner.

Peter Island Resort and Yacht Harbour has just 50 rooms, 30 on a spit of land looking out over the Sir Francis Drake Channel, and another 20 clustered at one end of Deadman's Bay. The Beach rooms at Deadman's Bay are spacious, with romantic bathtubs that open onto tropical greenery. There are four to a building, two upstairs and two downstairs. The lower units open right onto the beach and the upper units have higher ceilings, a bit more privacy, and more dramatic views. The rooms near the dock are smaller and are also four to a building. The first floor Garden View rooms look out across the pool or into the gardens. The second-floor Ocean View rooms look across the pool and gardens to the water. There are five beaches, a water sports program, a stunning swimming pool, tennis courts, a fitness trail, and an exercise room.

The Tradewinds Restaurant is a peaceful and elegant spot open to the island breezes. There is a buffet breakfast here daily. Dinner is a la carte and there is a different, and extensive, menu every night but Saturday, when there is a Grand Buffet. Deadman's Bay Bar and Grill is open every day for lunch and offers both a buffet and an a la carte menu. On season, dinner is usually served here six nights a week. Both restaurants are expensive. *52 units, 3 private villas. Rates including breakfast and dinner: $800-$930 ($490-$595 off-season) plus 10% service charge. Managing Director: Wayne Kafcsak. Reservations: 800-346-4451. Tel: 284-495-2000. Fax: 284-495-2500. P.O. Box 211.*

ONE PERFECT DAY IN PARADISE

An early wake up and a walk to watch the sun
rise out of the caribbean sea

A read and a rest until breakfast

some swimming, sunning, sailing or snorkeling

a light lunch by the water

a rest in your room

some biking or hiking or just exploring the
sights

a warm shower and change

a cool drink as the sun slips into the ocean

dinner, a dance, a dip in the pool

a stargazing trip to the beach

and back to the room for sweet dreams

Great things to do

Float - just lie on one of those wonderful floats in the warm Caribbean and do nothing, just float.

Walk on a beach at night - take in the sounds and sights, the stars, the moon, and look for the magic of the sparkling phosphorus at the water's edge.

Experience a sunrise along a beach - you don't have to do it the morning after your night beach walk, and you don't have to stay up all night. Just get up a little early (you can always go back to bed).

Do a Drive - pick one of the drives in this book or make one up, but do get up in the hills of Tortola or Virgin Gorda for some magnificent views.

Go somewhere in a boat - go anywhere or nowhere.

Spend an hour alone doing nothing - inside or out, day or night - no TV, no tapes, no writing, no reading, just you and yourself for an hour doing absolutely nothing.

Catch the BBC news from London - it's on ZBVI.

Take a day trip to another island - go to Jost or Anegada or Tortola or an uninhabited cay.

Go to a horse race - they're held once a month at the track at Sea Cow's Bay, and they're a lot of fun!

See the islands from the air - If you missed this because you arrived by ferry, then call Fly BVI so you won't miss the spectacular views from a plane!

10. TORTOLA

Beef Island

Long Bay (west)

Elizabeth Bay

Maya Cove

Josiah's Bay

Brandywine Bay

Brewer's Bay

Skyworld

Road Town & Harbour

Cane Garden Bay

Apple Bay

Long Bay

Smuggler's Bay

Frenchman's Cay

Soper's Hole

⇐ N

TORTOLA IN A NUTSHELL

Tortola is the largest British Virgin Island and exceptionally hilly. There is virtually no flat land. Houses are scattered on the steep hillsides and roads hug the shoreline or run feverishly up and down the island's multiple peaks showing off stunning, airplane-like views.

This island is by far the most populated British Virgin Island, with over 15,000 people (or over 80% of the entire BVI population). Nestled against Tortola's south shore is Road Town, the capital of the BVI.

Road Town, which is built almost entirely on reclaimed land, is the only real "town" in the entire country. Government buildings, plus grocery, plumbing, office supply, and hardware stores are mixed in with the bars, restaurants, shops, and marinas that are fun to visit. There's also a cruise ship dock, public ferry dock, and Customs Office.

At the west end of the island is West End, where there is a public ferry dock and Customs Office, plus a marina, some shops, and a Pusser's Restaurant and Store. The east end of the island, including Beef Island (which is only 600 feet from Tortola and the location of the airport), is less developed but has some excellent restaurants and shops.

The best beaches, some with little restaurants and bars, some completely undeveloped, are strung along Tortola's entire north shore.

WHAT YOU CAN DO ON TORTOLA

Swim, snorkel, hike, horseback ride, see stunning views, drive remarkably hilly roads, eat outside almost all the time — whether you're at a local "fish fry" or a fancy gourmet restaurant, drink barefoot at beachside bars, sample ales and beers in British pubs, rent a boat, take a boat ride . . . the list goes on and on. Shopping is on a small scale but there are great things to buy if you know where to look.

GETTING TO TORTOLA FROM NEARBY ISLANDS

Tortola is reachable by ferry from North Sound and The Valley on Virgin Gorda, Peter Island, Jost Van Dyke, and St. Thomas and St. John in the USVI. *(See page 121 for routes here from the U.S.)*

56

EXPLORING TORTOLA

Spectacular panoramic vistas are one of Tortola's most outstanding features. Although the roads are remarkably steep in places, many people will want to rent a car and drive, at least once, to catch these stunning views. If you are truly faint of heart, you can take a taxi tour.

TORTOLA'S AMAZING ROADS

On Tortola, there's almost no such thing as a straight, flat piece of road. This mountainous island isn't a single steep mound, but rather a collection of many, many knobby hilltops. Tortola's road system is draped over these knobs, dropping swiftly to sea level every once in a while to skirt a shimmering bay or run along a crescent of beach.

The roads themselves are astonishing: a collection of hairpin turns and dizzying descents and ascents that often are bordered by precipitous drops. Because of this, Tortola's scenery is especially spectacular from a car. When you are driving on this island you are constantly changing altitude and frequently looking across plummeting valleys to other hilltops, with sweeping views of the sea and other islands beyond. There are many views from over 1000 feet.

Car and Jeep Rentals: In Road Town, delightful Ms. Burke at **ITGO** (494-2639) on Wickham's Cay I is the person to see. At West End, **Hertz** (495-4405), right next to the Jolly Roger, is a good bet. You'll need a temporary BVI license (which you can't get without showing your valid license from home), which costs $10 and is easily available through the rental agency. And remember, driving is on the left.

Taxi Tours: Almost any taxi will take you around part or all of the island for about $45. Wheatley's has excellent service. Call 494-3357 and ask for "Fix-It" — he's the boss and whatever kind of tour you want, he'll "fix it" for you.

> "The roads are astonishing: a collection of hairpin turns and dizzying descents and ascents bordered by precipitous drops."

57

HINTS FOR DRIVING ON TORTOLA

✓ Driving is on the left. This is the trickiest when you are turning from one road onto another or heading into a round-a-bout. Invent a reminder, like staying on the same side of the road as your heart.

✓ Try to share the driving. Managing the roads requires constant attention, so whoever is driving misses the views.

✓ It can help to keep track, on a map, of where you think you are so you'll recognize a turn. There are few road signs and the twists and turns happen fast.

✓ On steep hills, in automatic cars, if you can't get enough power, even in low gear, turn off the air conditioning and you'll be okay.

✓ Hills and curves look completely different from the other direction, so a road you have just driven can look totally unfamiliar on the return trip. Don't feel stupid. It happens to everybody.

✓ Beware those tight little curves you see on a map — those are hills! However, distances are short, and almost everything is only ten minutes away from the last thing, even if it is over switchbacks.

✓ Tailgaters are common, and can hang unnervingly close behind you. If they annoy you, pull to the side and let them pass. When you tire of doing this, just stop looking in the rear view mirror.

✓ Speaking of mirrors, keep a lookout for mirrors on hills and curves. These are specially positioned to give you a view of oncoming traffic that you can't otherwise see.

✓ When you encounter goats, cows, or sheep being herded along the road, just slow down and politely make your way through. Watch also for the stray goat, or cow, or horse that is standing in the road intently munching on the leaves of an overhanging tree branch.

✓ Do be very careful. "Island time" doesn't seem to apply to driving here and you'll encounter Indianapolis 500 wanna-bes.

A SPECTACULAR
TEN MINUTE DRIVE
FROM ROAD TOWN TO SKYWORLD

This drive takes you on an ear-popping 1300 foot ascent in about eight breathtaking minutes. It's an awesome trip in both directions. At the top is an observation deck with the highest 360 degree view in the BVI. It's possible to see Anegada and even St. Croix which is 40 miles away. There's also a great restaurant, Skyworld, and a neat little shop.

Time: 10 minutes each way, plus however long you stay mesmerized by the view.
When to do this: On clear days you can see the farthest. Sunsets here are gorgeous.

From Pusser's in Road Town, head east from the waterfront (the water is on your right) toward the center of Road Town. Stay on this road several minutes, until you come to a round-a-bout. Bear left, into the round-a-bout, and take your very first left out of the round-a-bout. You'll come to a "T" in the road. Turn right (keeping, of course, to the left side of the road). Take your first real left, which will head up hill. Sometimes this road sign says Joe's Hill Road, sometimes it says Cane Garden Bay, and sometimes it's not there. Once you've turned, those on the right side of the car can start looking for some great views of Road Town and Road Harbour.

After some sharp twists back and forth, there is an extremely severe switchback curve that climbs up at an almost impossible angle. (Your ears should have popped by now.) The switchback spits you out onto an almost level bit of road. Bear right after you pass a white two-story building on your left.

Soon you'll see a spectacular view of neighboring islands on the left. There are several little pull-off areas on your left where you can stop to look at the views and take photographs.

Watch for the sign to Skyworld. It's on the left but the turn is actually to the right, and it's an extremely sharp turn that also heads up. After you turn right, you'll pass an elementary school (imagine going to school every day and having these views out your window!) and then you'll be on a narrow ridge with a pasture sweeping down to your left. Just ahead is a hill.

Now is the time to look for the entrance to Skyworld. The sign isn't always there but it's your first left and it is steep. Drive straight up until you are spilled out onto a little plateau with a parking lot. Pull in, get out, and enjoy the view.

From here, looking south, you can see the entire chain of islands that border the Sir Francis Drake Channel. From left to right, they are the south end of Virgin Gorda, Fallen Jerusalem, Round Rock (the little one), Ginger, Cooper, Salt, Peter, Norman, and tiny Pelican Island. The small island farthest to the right is the easternmost USVI which is called Flanagan Island.

For a lunch or beverage with a great view, head to the entrance of the building, which is the Skyworld Restaurant. To reach the observation deck, follow the path just to the right of the restaurant entrance, which leads around to a set of stairs.

RETURNING FROM SKYWORLD
Retracing your steps is easy except for one place. After you've turned right out of the Skyworld driveway, and turned left after the school, you'll be on level road for a while. Watch for the white two-story house and take the abrupt left just before the house. Be prepared for some truly spectacular airplane-like views as you drop about 1100 feet in the four or five minutes it takes to get back to sea level. To get back to the round-a-bout when you reach the bottom of this amazing hill, go left and then take your first right. Follow it to the end, turn left, and you'll be back in the round-a-bout.

"Be prepared for some truly spectacular airplane-like views as you drop about 1100 feet in the four or five minutes it takes to get back to sea level."

TORTOLA'S TOWNS

If you look at Tortola's curvy shoreline from a plane, you'll see that it is defined by one bay after another. These bays have become Tortola's "landmarks" and the names of Tortola's settlements. People live in Sea Cows Bay, or Carrot Bay, or Baughers Bay, or Soper's Hole. The bays are used to indicate location and you will encounter bay names far more frequently than road names when you ask for directions.

The three largest towns are Road Town, West End (also referred to as Soper's Hole or Frenchman's Cay), and East End.

SHOPPING IN ROAD TOWN

There are many wonderful places to shop in Road Town but they are scattered about (although within easy walking distance from each other). Bear in mind that this is the capital of a country and also the country's biggest town. Islanders come here from all over Tortola and from all of the other British Virgin Islands for almost everything they need — from hammers to scotch tape to drivers' licenses.

Road Town has no separate "tourist" area with a nice little row of boutiques and eateries. It is a real place, with restaurants, bars, and shops tucked in between hardware stores and government agencies. The islanders dress up when they come to Road Town because it is their "city." It's okay for visitors to be casually dressed but bathing suits or short shorts in town are unacceptable. Also, don't be intimidated by a shabby storefront door. Paint and metal are simply no match for the Caribbean sun, wind, and salt air.

GREAT ROAD TOWN SHOPS

There are two main shopping areas in Road Town: Main Street and Wickham's Cay I. Locals use landmarks for directions so it really helps to know the major ones. In Road Town, when you ask where something is, it's usually near the "Chase Bank" or the "round-a-bout" or "Bobby's" (a supermarket) or "Bolo's" (which is next to Bobby's). Bolo's, by the way, is an excellent source for everything from batteries to cosmetics to office supplies.

61

Main Street Shops

Buccaneer's Bounty (494-7510) specializes in terrific gifts with a nautical theme and tropical gifts and has the island's best collection of greeting cards!

Caribbean Handprints (494-3717) features pastel silk-screen fabrics, sold by the yard or fashioned into clothing, beach bags, place mats, and more. Bring home a soft kimono and remember the BVI every morning!

Esme's Shop (494-3961) is the place to come when you start feeling "out of touch." There's a huge selection of U.S. newspapers and magazines.

Island Treasures (495-4787), which is actually near the hospital on Waterfront Drive, has a large collection of decorative houseware accessories, lots of incense and candles, plus an appealing selection of prints.

Jewellery Box (494-7278) features gold and silver jewelry and one-of-a-kind pieces fashioned out of shells, wood, and the local sandbox plant.

Ooh La La (494-2433) may be tiny and but it's jammed full of surprises, from games to t-shirts to potholders!

Pusser's Company Store (494-2467) carries attractive, wearable clothing for the whole family, bottles of their famous rum, nautical antiques, island books, postcards, and much, much more!

Samarkand (494-6415) hand-crafts gold and silver jewelry. Many pieces have an island motif — sand dollars, shells, anchors — and make perfect gifts.

Sea Urchin (494-2044) is a delightful place to come for fashionable sportswear, beachwear, sandals, beach bags, local books, and fun things for the whole family. (This shop is actually on Waterfront Drive, next to Capriccio di Mare. There are also branches at Wickhams Cay I and West End.)

Shops Around the Corner on Main Street

Caribbean Fine Arts, Ltd. (494-4240) carries an array of watercolors and prints by local artists. Sylvia, the owner, also does a fine job of framing.

Fort Wines Gourmet (494-3036) has a remarkable selection of fine wines and champagnes and gourmet specialty items. You'll find Petrossian caviars, Hediard delicacies, fine chocolates, confitures, and terrines. You can also stop here for an espresso or glass of champagne or a light lunch.

J. R. O'Neal (494-2292) sells brightly-colored Mexican glassware, handpainted ceramic tableware from Spain and Italy, fabrics from India, and cotton rugs.

Heritage Book Shop (494-5879) specializes in Caribbean books.

Latitude 18 (494-4807) carries colorful sportswear and island wear.

Sunny Caribbee Herb and Spice Co. (494-2178) is the place for wonderful exotic spices, "hangover cures," ceramics, books, cookbooks, and island art.

Serendipity (494-5865) features an eclectic mix of island sundresses, delicate hand-painted glass, hand-painted t-shirts, and local handicrafts.

Sunny Caribbee Gallery (494-2178) is a showcase for prints, water colors, and oil paintings by artists from all over the Caribbean.

Turtle Dove (494-3611) carries fine china, swimwear, silk dresses, and French perfumes.

Shopping on Wickhams Cay I
Learn and Fun Shop (494-3856) has a huge variety of games and toys for kids of all ages.

Sea Urchin (494-4108), in the old Mill, carries an inexhaustible supply of sandals, beachwear, resortwear, sundresses, sunglasses, and books for the whole family. Other branches are on Waterfront Drive and at West End.

Violet's (494-6398) specializes in beautiful imported designer lingerie and accessories and shopping here is the "good news" for any woman whose luggage went elsewhere.

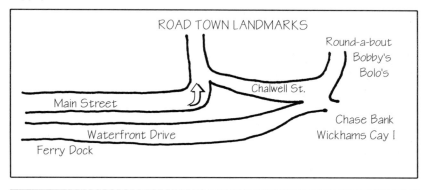

SHOPPING IN WEST END

West End refers to the area along the shore of Soper's Hole, a deep anchorage at the West End of Tortola. The Customs Office, public ferry docks, Zelma's Variety, and the Jolly Roger Bar and Restaurant are on one side of the harbour.

On the other side (which is actually an island called Frenchman's Cay that is connected to the mainland by a bridge) is a small group of shops, art galleries, a great hair salon, and a Pusser's Restaurant and Store.

*When you feel like food or a drink, stop at **Pusser's** for a salad or sandwich or their famous Painkiller Punch or head over to the **Jolly Roger** (you'll want to drive or taxi — it's about a mile) for great breakfasts and delicious pizza, cracked conch, and hamburgers.*

Ample Hamper (495-4684) sells all kinds of groceries, including fresh produce, liquor, and cheeses.

Caribbean Corner Spice House (495-4498) packages their own spices, hot sauces, island soaps, jams, and teas, including bush teas.

Pusser's Company Store (495-4554) carries clothing for the whole family, their famous rum, nautical items, and island books.

Sea Urchin (495-4850) stocks lots and lots of shoes, sandals, bathing suits, beachwear, sundresses, t-shirts, and books. There are two other branches of this terrific store in Road Town.

Waves (495-4208) is the best hair salon on the island, or perhaps in the world! Come here for a really great haircut — men or women.

Zenida (495-4867) features exotic items from all over the world — colorful fabrics, bedspreads, sarongs, wood carvings, unusual jewelry, carry-alls, and much more.

And not far from Frenchman's Cay, over Zion Hill Road and worth the drive, the **Long Bay Beach Resort** (495-4252) has a charming two-story boutique that carries Caribbean art, a wide selection of resortwear and accessories, current books, and handsome t-shirts.

TORTOLA'S PEOPLE

When frequent visitors to the BVI are asked why they keep coming back and what is so special about these islands, a common answer to both questions is "The People."

A handful of the people who make Tortola special are noted below. The omissions obviously far outnumber the inclusions, but following are a few "front of the house" people that make visitors happy they chose the BVI.

Dennis at The Pub
Ms. Burke at ITGO in Road Town
Sylvia at Caribbean Fine Arts
Jim and Vince at Skyworld
Lillian at Pusser's Road Town Store
James and Ernest and Wayne at Long Bay
Cele and Davide at Brandywine Bay
Vernon Dawson at the Conch Shell
Restaurant
Mrs. Davis at the LEARN & FUN shop
Massage Therapist Cynthia Wilson
Sheppard of Sheppard Power Boats
Claris Francis at Liat
Noel and Sylvester and Tom
and Frank for a taxi
Quito
Ruben
Al Frett
and there are many, many more

TORTOLA'S BEST BEACHES

Tortola's best beaches run along all of the island's north shore. It's here that you will find picture-perfect stretches of glistening white sand bordered by sea grapes and palm trees. Some are very easy to reach. Others have bumpy and steep approaches. You may be the only one on the beach and there are no lifeguards so do be careful when swimming.

Apple Bay, in front of Bomba's near Long Bay, is the most popular surfing beach as it gets long rollers coming in from the Atlantic.

Brewer's Bay is a long and bumpy ride down but worth the discomfort. It's a calm beach great for swimming and snorkeling. The access from Ridge Road, just east of the Cool Breeze Bar, is the easiest approach.

Cane Garden Bay is the closest beach to Road Town (just 15 minutes) even though it's on the north shore. Because it is so accessible and so famous, it can just be too crowded some days on season. Definitely skip it when cruise ships are in Road Town. It's too picturesque to miss completely, so try stopping by in the early morning or evening or anytime off season. To get there from Road Town, just follow the directions to Skyworld (page 59) but go straight instead of right when you see the first Skyworld sign and follow the road down to sea level.

Elizabeth Beach is a good swimming beach on Tortola's East End. It's also very pretty. To get there go to the Police Station in Long Look, turn onto Blackburn Highway, and then right onto Greenland Road. Go up a hill and look for a gate on the left (you're free to open it — all beaches in the BVI are public). Watch out for strong undertows.

Josiah's Bay Beach is often completely deserted. Some days this east end beach can have strong undertows. Follow Little Dick's Road from the Long Look Police Station and go right at the sign (before the hill).

Long Bay Beach (East) is actually on Beef Island and is long and lovely and good for swimming. Head toward the airport but turn left when you see the salt flats and then follow the dirt road to the right which curves around the flats (and please don't drive across the flats).

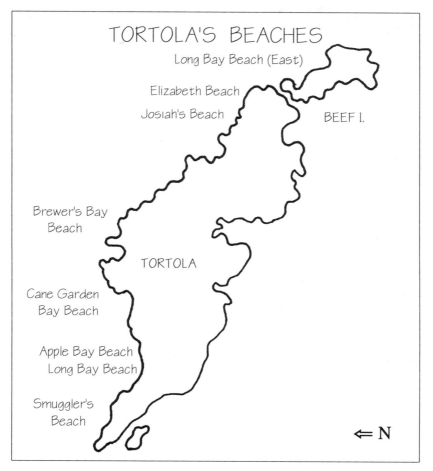

Long Bay Beach (West) is a stunning mile-long stretch of white sand that is never crowded. Tortola's best resort, Long Bay Beach Resort, fronts part of it and has a nice beach restaurant and bar.

Smuggler's Cove takes a bit of bouncing around to get to but it's one of Tortola's most picture-perfect beaches. A wide crescent of white sand wraps along most of the shore and the water is the color of turquoise neon light. This bay is almost always calm and on some days can be as still as a pond. The bottom is sandy and deepens very gradually. *(See page 74 for a more complete description.)*

THINGS THAT ARE FUN
TO DO ON TORTOLA

❑Go to the airport and watch the little planes land and take off. The Tortola-Beef Island airport has a great observation deck.

❑Visit the Botanic Gardens in Road Town (across from the Police Station). They're open daily from 8 am to 6 pm and you'll see all kinds of flowers and plants and a special section on medicinal plants.

❑Go to a local sporting event. Check the local papers or stop by the Tourist Board in Road Town to see what is going on. There can be softball games, rugby matches, horse races, and sailing regattas.

❑Head to the docks and watch the boats come and go. You'll see vessels of all sizes, both power and sail. It's fun to watch the skilled skippers navigate so effortlessly, and even more fun to watch some of the less-experienced charterers try to manage. In Road Town, go to Village Cay Marina or the Moorings . At West End, go to Pusser's on Frenchman's Cay.

❑Drive or take a taxi to the observation platform at Skyworld. It is less than ten minutes from Road Town and the views are unmatchable. Bring your camera and just keep shooting. This is the highest unobstructed 360 degree view in the BVI.

❑Go horseback riding. Shadow (494-2262) and Mr. Thomas (494-4442) have great guided riding trips into the hills and down to the beaches.

GREAT WATER SPORTS

Cane Garden Bay on Tortola and Trellis Bay on Beef Island are two very protected bays and are the two most popular areas for windsurfing, kayaking, and sunfishing. You can also go water-skiing on Cane Garden Bay and parasailing at West End. On calm days it is wonderful fun to rent your own little powerboat and go wherever you want. You can rent them at Cane Garden Bay and West End.

WINDSURFING, WATER-SKIING, KAYAKING, AND PARASAILING

Cane Garden Bay Pleasure Boats (495-9660) rents Hobie Cats, sailboats, sunfish, windsurfers, kayaks, canoes, and snorkel equipment. Prices range from $15 an hour for a sunfish to $25 an hour for a Hobie Cat. You can go water-skiing for $50 a half hour or $75 an hour.

Boardsailing BVI (495-2447) at Trellis Bay on Beef Island rents equipment by the hour, day, and week, and offers all levels of instruction.

Parasail BVI (495-4967), at Soper's Hole, takes you up 600' for a bird's-eye view of some spectacular scenery for $50 a ride.

RENTING LITTLE POWERBOATS

Cane Garden Bay Pleasure Boats (495-9660) rents 18'-24' powerboats with a bimini, cooler, and ship-to-shore radio for $150-$300 a day, including fuel.

Sheppard Powerboat Rentals (495-4099) operates out of Soper's Hole and rents Mako 23'-26' power boats with a center console and bimini for $150-$250 per day plus fuel. A captain is $85 additional per day.

HAVE LUNCH OR DINNER ON ANOTHER ISLAND!

If you want to go to Cooper or Jost Van Dyke or any other island for dinner (or for the day), or if you need transportation to another island and want to take a water taxi, just call **Sheppard Power Boat Rentals and Water Taxis** (495-4099).

GREAT SNORKEL TRIPS AND BOAT TRIPS TO OTHER ISLANDS

Remarkably, from Tortola, it's only three to five miles to all the other British Virgin Islands, except far flung Anegada, and there are excellent boat trips available to all the islands, even Anegada. For a very reasonable price you can go with a group or charter a small boat with a captain. These trips leave from Road Town or Soper's Hole at West End. Almost all take all major credit cards.

Most boat trips head to other islands and to several great snorkeling spots. Exactly where they go will depend on the weather, and especially on how windy it is. Some of these trips stop at a restaurant on an island and others serve lunch on board.

If you know how to handle boats and prefer to be in charge, you can also rent a little powerboat and take yourself on your own snorkel trip. It's best to do this when the weather is calm. Call Sheppard at Sheppard Powerboat Rentals (495-4099) or Ash Harrigan at Power Boat Rentals, Ltd. (494-5511).

What to bring? Towel and bathing suit, sunscreen, your own snorkel gear if you have a prescription mask, camera, and film.

BOAT TRIPS THAT LEAVE FROM ROAD TOWN

Speedy's Ferry Service (495-5240) offers a day trip to Virgin Gorda from Road Town which includes transportation to The Baths and lunch at the Bath & Turtle Restaurant. No advance reservation is needed. Just be there before 9 am and be sure the boat you get on is Speedy's, not Smith's. The boat leaves at 9 am from the public ferry dock in Road Town and leaves Virgin Gorda for the trip back at 3:30 pm (4:00 Sunday). Cost is $30 a person ($22 for children).

Cat PPALU (496-7716) is the BVI's largest catamaran and it heads to different islands on different days. Although there can be as many as 20 people, you'll usually be with less than 12. On Saturdays (and sometimes Wednesdays on season) it's off to Anegada at 8:30 am. It's a three hour sail each way but there is still time to snorkel at Anegada's Loblolly Bay and have a great lobster lunch before making the return trip, which usually gets back about 6 pm. Other days the boat heads to The Baths on Virgin Gorda and the Caves at Norman.

Caves at Norman. Some days you are taken to a restaurant and other days lunch is served on board. Jamaican jerk chicken, salads, pumpkin muffins, and freshly baked chocolate chip cookies are chef specialties. Rates are $65 per person ($85 with a lobster lunch for Anegada), less off season.

Goddess Athena (494-0000), an 84' ketch, is known as the "little pirate ship" and is one of the most famous charter boats in the Caribbean. This spacious luxury vessel specializes in elegant day-sail "excursion cruises" to islands around Tortola. Appealing day trips range from a Jost Van Dyke Lobster Feast to Snorkeling at Cooper Island to Around Tortola in a Day. They also do evening champagne cruises and seasonal "theme" cruises. Prices range from $45 to $120 per person.

White Squall II (494-2564) heads to the Baths on Virgin Gorda and Cooper Island or goes to Norman Island and the Indians. It's a traditional 80' schooner so there may be a lot of people but there is still plenty of room. Rates include a barbecue lunch with wine, rum punch, and beer, and complimentary snorkel equipment. The boat sails at 9:30 am from Village Cay Marina in Road Town. Rates are $85 per person.

Captain Roy (494-1147) takes people on half and full day snorkeling trips all over the BVI on his 34' snorkeling boat. Trips start from Prospect Reef Resort. He's incredibly knowledgeable, known for his teaching abilities, and happy to teach kids of all ages. Half day trips go to the Indians and Norman, or Salt Island and the Wreck of the Rhone plus Cooper and are from 9 am-12:30 pm and 1:30-5 pm. Full days (9:30 am-5:00 pm and 3 snorkelings) can be your choice of The Baths, on to North Sound, and then snorkeling at one of the Dogs, or to Jost Van Dyke via Sandy Cay and Green Cay. (On this trip he can pick you up at West End.) Half days are $30 a person. Full days are $50 a person, not including lunch.

Dual Bliss (496-7149) is for those who want to combine excellent, out-of-the-way snorkeling trips with fine cuisine. Bill and Louise take two to four people (six maximum) on a very personalized trip to very special snorkel spots where most people don't go. For lunch, enjoy Louise's tasty version of chicken marsala plus salad, wine, and homemade bread, and brie and fruit later in the afternoon. Rates are $100 per person (2 people minimum) on season and $90 off-season.

Patouche II (494-6300) offers snorkeling trips to nearby islands via catamaran and includes guided underwater tours and snorkel instruction. This is a good trip for people who have never snorkeled, but seasoned snorkelers will also enjoy it because of the destinations. Choose between a half day and one snorkel spot or a full day and two snorkel spots plus lunch. In either case, you'll be with 6 to 16 other people. They usually go snorkeling near Norman, Cooper, and Peter. Rates per person are $68 half day (two snorkel sites) and $98 for a full day (three snorkel sites and lunch).

Silmaril (495-9225) is a 41' sailing yacht based at Peter Island. Paul and Judy will come pick you up anywhere on the south side of Tortola for a day (or half day) of whatever you want to do. They are happy to let you tailor the trip but they'll make suggestions or plan it for you if you wish. You can decide whether you want to eat on board or at a beach bar or gourmet restaurant and whether you want to spend more time sailing or resting at anchor or snorkeling. There is a two person minimum and rates are $380 per day for two people, and $95 per person for four, five, or six people. Half days (which can be morning, afternoon, or into sunset) are $260 for two people, $30 each additional person. Overnight charters are $695 per night (two night minimum) including meals and beverages.

BOAT TRIPS THAT LEAVE FROM WEST END

Kuralu (495-4381) is a 50' luxury cruising catamaran that is so popular it's booked almost every day. Robin Pinfold is the owner and captain, and his charming golden retriever is often first mate! This is a fine trip for families and children as there is safety netting around the boat (Robin has a young son who is usually in school). Choose from two trips. One goes to Green Cay for snorkeling and then makes a great spinnaker sail to Jost Van Dyke. After lunch on board, you can swim or snorkel and stop at Foxy's before the return sail. The other trip goes to the Indians for snorkeling and to Benures Bay where you can swim with big turtles. Lunch is usually several salads, quiche, a variety of cheeses and cold meats, and french bread. Since Robin is usually out every day, just leave a message on his machine saying where, and when, you want to go, the number of people, and where you are staying. He'll be sure to get back to you that evening. Trips are around $75 per person (around $35 for children under 12).

Remember, the Caribbean sun is stronger than up north — wear a hat and lots of sun block on your nautical adventure! And don't forget your camera.

FITNESS AND LAND SPORTS ON TORTOLA

HORSEBACK RIDING
Both Shadow and Mr. Ellis have very gentle horses and will take two to six people on guided rides to Brewer's Bay, Cane Garden Bay, and along Ridge Road. Instruction is also available. Call Shadow at **Shadow's Stables** (494-2262) on Ridge Road just east of Skyworld or Mr. Thomas, who runs the **Ellis Thomas Riding School** (494-4442) at the Race Track at Sea Cow's Bay. Do wear long pants.

TENNIS
You'll find six courts and tennis pro Mike Adamson at **Prospect Reef Resort** (495-3311) and three courts at the **Long Bay Beach Resort** (495-4252) and non-hotel guests are welcome at both for a nominal charge.

THERAPEUTIC MASSAGE
There are two excellent trained specialists in therapeutic massage. At **Fort Recovery** (495-4467), Pamelah Jacobson specializes in a combination of Swedish, Shiatsu, and Reflexology massage. **Cynthia Wilson** (494-5999) also specializes in a combination of Swedish, Shiatsu, and Reflexology massage and focuses on sports injuries. Be sure to call for appointments 24 hours in advance.

AEROBIC CLASSES
Mike and Lisa offer daily aerobic exercise classes and body conditioning classes and ballet and gymnastic classes for kids at **Body Images at Healthy Prospect Centre** (494-3299). Call for schedules.

YOGA CLASSES
Yoga classes are given by appointment (24-hour notice please) at **Fort Recovery** (495-4467).

HIKING
Trails to Sage Mountain National Park show off a great view from the highest point on Tortola, 1780 feet. You can also hike from Brewer's Bay to Mt. Healthy National Park where there is a restored 18th-century windmill. It's a great place for a picnic.

A "SMUGGLER'S" ADVENTURE

Smuggler's Cove is an out-of-the-way, beautiful beach with good snorkeling and calm water for swimming. It's on the northwest shore of Tortola and about eight very bumpy minutes from the Long Bay Beach Resort.

What you need to bring: swim suit, towel, snorkeling gear, single dollar bills and quarters for the "honor" beach bar.

Smuggler's Cove: This is one of Tortola's most beautiful and most protected beaches. There is a good snorkeling reef which you can easily spot from land. The best snorkeling is out from the shore a bit, just before the little waves are breaking.

Through the sea grape trees in the center of the beach is a rather unusual beach bar. Outside is a small cannon but probably what you'll notice first is the old Lincoln Continental which is placed prominently among the tables and chairs scattered about the bar.

This is a serve-yourself honor snack bar. On the long wooden bar, among a collection of bottles and shells washed up from the sea, is a handwritten sign that presents the menu and price list. It's next to the cash register, which is actually a cigar box.

You can get beer, sodas, cans of potato stix, oreo cookies, and your choice of two postcards, and you can rent beach chairs. Everything costs a multiple of $.50 (beers are $2), so it's usually easy to make change from the money in the cigar box. Tipping, the sign says, is not necessary.

Decide what you want, put your money in the cigar box (making change if necessary), and serve yourself. The cans of potato stix and cookies are right on the bar. If you want cold drinks, head to the kitchen, which is through the door past the bar, and look in various refrigerators until you find what you want. If you're interested in island history, check to see if the owner is around (he's a spritely and distinguished gentleman who is sometimes wearing a pith helmet). He is a great source of recent island history (he also used to make tasty

74

toasted cheese sandwiches but he's doing that no longer). Queen Elizabeth actually rode in the Lincoln Continental that is sitting in the restaurant. She was driven in it around Tortola in 1977, when she was celebrating the 25th anniversary of her coronation.

Directions: Get yourself to Long Bay Beach Resort. The road from here to Smuggler's is almost all dirt but passable (although not necessarily comfortable because of the bumps) in a car. If there has been a lot of rain and it appears to be very muddy, you'll want a jeep-type vehicle with a lot of clearance. The drive only takes about eight minutes but it will seem longer the first time.

Follow the road past Long Bay Beach Resort. After the last pink buildings the road veers abruptly left. Start driving up the hill but look for the very first right. It's hard to spot because you've got your eyes on what's ahead, and the turn is abrupt and drops sharply down. However, it's just before the sign for Belmont Estates. (This is one of the most exclusive areas of Tortola and there are many luxurious homes and villas tucked up in these hills.)

Take this right, which spills quickly down. Be patient and go slowly. The road ahead is dirt, deeply rutted, and has giant potholes and rocks that can blow a tire, so you have to kind of pick your way around obstacles.

This road winds through tangles of second-growth forest and is woodsy and shady. Don't worry that you can't see any water. You're driving inland a bit to get around a large salt pond. Just after you spot it, the road will bear right and you'll be in the parking area for Smuggler's Cove. You may see a few other cars, but if you are lucky, you could be the only one. Park along either side of the road.

Occasionally, production companies from around the world use this beach for a movie or a commercial so on rare occasions you may come upon a camera crew, but there will still be plenty of empty beach.

Driving back from Smuggler's
Returning is a little more difficult than driving to Smuggler's because there are several turns that lead to nowhere but that look seductively "right." Just keep bearing left whenever you have a choice and eventually you will be back on the road that leads past Long Bay. (Except don't take the very last left — when you spot a concrete road ahead of you heading up an incline and there is a house above you on the right.)

SOME TIPS ON
BVI RESTAURANTS

❑Don't be alarmed if there aren't many other patrons in a restaurant. In the U.S. this generally means that you are in a bad place, but in the islands it is perfectly normal. In the islands there are just far fewer people around.

❑Contrary to popular thought, vegetables and fruits are not plentiful on these islands. (The rains are too uneven, the land too rocky.) Virtually all produce is shipped from the southern Caribbean, Puerto Rico, or from the States. If there is very little lettuce in your salad, it's probably because the restaurant is desperately awaiting a fresh shipment.

❑Fresh milk is shipped from St. Thomas and Puerto Rico and quickly turns in the Caribbean heat. Although you will see fresh milk in the supermarkets, virtually everyone relies on "Long Life" milk which comes in non-refrigerated cartons and is usually from England.

❑Many visitors from the U.S. get frustrated by the peaceful pace of restaurant service, forgetting, of course, that the reason they came to the BVI in the first place was to slow down and relax. Enjoy the scenery and the pace. If you have to catch a plane or a boat, let someone know and they'll happily serve you more quickly.

❑Water is scarce on these islands. Islanders can last a week with the water people from the U.S. can waste in a day. Drinking water is rarely served unless requested.

❑Many restaurants serve American-style food, but it won't necessarily be exactly what you are expecting. Cooking styles are different here and supplies are limited.

TORTOLA'S GREAT RESTAURANTS AND BARS

One of the extraordinary things about dining in the islands is that most of the time you are outside. Many restaurants simply don't have walls. A canopy or roof protects you from the occasional cloudburst. In addition, many overlook the water. It is possible to get anything from a sandwich to an elegant, four course meal in this kind of exotic setting. Restaurants below are organized into the categories of fine dining, casual dining, pubs, and where to find great local food. All are open for lunch and dinner unless otherwise noted. See map for locations.

TORTOLA'S ELEGANT RESTAURANTS
Virtually all of Tortola's finer restaurants have a menu that could be called "Continental and/or French with a West Indian splash." You'll find fresh local fish as well as high-quality imported steaks and chops, frequently served with West Indian-style sauces, or sauces and salsas made with local ingredients. You'll also get a taste of local fruits and vegetables. Entrees run about $18 to $30. Dress is smart casual (no tank-tops, no shorts).

Brandywine Bay Restaurant (495-2301), an easy ten minute cab ride from Road Town, is perhaps the BVI's finest restaurant. You can dine by candlelight inside or on a romantic terrace looking out over the ocean. Italian owner/chef Davide Pugliese flies in ingredients from all over the world, buys the best local fish, and makes his own mozzarella. The ever-changing menu offers a number of appetizers, entrees, and dessert choices nightly and this is the place to come if you like fresh mussels, tomato bread soup, Peking roast duck with passionfruit, grilled porterhouse steak, stuffed veal chops, grilled fresh tuna, lemon tarts, and chocolate walnut torte served in an elegant, sophisticated setting. The wine list includes excellent Italian and Australian selections. *Dinner only. Closed Sundays and also early-August to mid-October.*

Callaloo (494-3311), at Prospect Reef Resort, is a peaceful second-floor spot overlooking a small harbor. Ocean breezes waft through the large open windows. Highlights here include the cracked jerk conch, callaloo pepperpot soup, grilled shrimp over pasta, and Caribbean-style Beef Wellington (a filet wrapped in sweet potato and callaloo). If you've saved room for dessert, have the rum cheese cake or sweet caramel custard.

77

Captain's Table (494-3885), in Road Town, offers fine dining either inside or outside along their veranda overlooking the harbor. The French chef has created a menu of French and Continental selections or you can choose a fresh lobster from their lobster pool. (Watch out you don't fall in — it's right in the floor in the middle of the dining room.) *No lunch weekends.*

The Garden at **Long Bay Beach Resort** (495-4252), on Tortola's West End, offers an elegant setting. Tables are on several levels, all lit by candles and open to the breezes. Come here for broiled local swordfish with pecan-lime butter, veal tenderloin with mushrooms, and a superb filet mignon with a red pepper salsa. Vegetarian entrees change nightly but the pasta pomodoro with basil is delicious. The wine list is varied. You might want to arrive early to enjoy a beverage on the adjoining, very pleasant garden terrace. On Tuesdays a buffet is served to the sound of a steel band and on Friday a fungi band accompanies a West Indian buffet. *Dinner only. Closed some Tuesdays and Fridays off-season.*

Skyworld (494-3567), about 10 minutes straight up from Road Town on Ridge Road, is an elegant, airy spot to dine. Windows show off stunning views. Jim and Vince turn out excellent cuisine including French tomato soup, local lobster au gratin, mushrooms stuffed with conch, steak Diane, and a filet mignon with an exceptional port wine sauce. Be sure to check out the napkins, which are folded differently on every table. The food is excellent all the time, but if you care about the view, get here before dark. The lunch menu is much simpler, with pumpkin soup, hamburgers, and sandwiches and salads the fare.

Sugar Mill (495-4355), in Apple Bay, is a romantic spot. The setting is lovely, in a restored 360 year old sugar mill with beautiful stonework walls and tables lit by candles. The menu changes nightly, with a choice of several appetizers, salads, entrees (including a vegetarian one), and desserts. Sweet potato soup, conch terrine, and smoked salmon corncakes are typical appetizers, and for the main course, grilled local fish with Creole sauce, roasted pepper-stuffed pork tenderloin, and quail with mango sauce. Come early for a drink in the lovely outdoor gazebo. *Dinner only. Closed August and September.*

"There is nothing which has yet been contrived by man by which so much happiness is produced as by a good tavern or inn"
— or a Tortola restaurant or bar.

— logical update of
Dr. Johnson's oft-quoted comment

GREAT CASUAL RESTAURANTS

Many casual restaurants are open-air and you can sit with a simple sandwich and a beer and enjoy an impossibly beautiful view. Hamburgers and sandwiches will be under $10, grilled fish or steak $15-$20. Lobster is always expensive. Dress is very casual but no bare feet unless you are headed to a beach bar. Places below are organized by location.

In and near Road Town

C&F (494-4941) at Purcell Estate just outside Road Town is run by Clarence, a well-known and very talented local chef and his wife, Florence, and it's packed nightly. People come for grilled fresh local swordfish and lobster, tasty barbecue ribs, fried plantains, conch fritters, and curry. *Dinner only.*

Cafesito (494-7412), on Waterfront Drive, is the place to head for a bottle of wine and a meal of assorted hot and cold Spanish-style tapas or a spicy chorizo sausage paella, seared tuna, and grilled N.Y. strip. *Closed Sundays.*

Capriccio di Mare (494-5369), on Waterfront Drive, is an authentic outdoor Italian cafe and the cuisine here is superb. In the morning sip espresso and munch on Italian pastries. Come back around noon for an Insalata Mista, penne Ammatriciana or another excellent pasta dish and return in the evening for a pizze margherita! The house specialty is a delicious Mango Bellini, a variation of the Bellini cocktail served at Harry's Bar in Venice. Owners are Davide and Cele Pugliese of Brandywine Bay fame. *Open 8 am to 9 pm. Closed Sundays.*

Lime 'n' Mango (494-2501), at Treasure Isle Hotel, has a superb view of Road Harbour through the treetops. Sunday through Friday there's good Mexican food — the fajitas are the best! Saturday there's a barbecue and a local band. Lunch is sandwiches and salads. *Breakfast also.*

The Fishtrap (494-3626), right behind Village Cay, serves burgers and salads for lunch and grilled fish and steaks for dinner on their breezy outdoor terrace.

The Pub (494-2608), right across from Fort Burt, has a pleasant veranda overlooking Road Harbour and the views are great day and night. Come here for barbequed ribs and chicken, sauteed or curried conch, fish and chips, caesar salad, and cheeseburgers and stop by in the morning for great pancakes.

Spaghetti Junction (494-4880), near the Cruise Ship Dock, has long been one of Tortola's most popular spots. Come for Italian classics like lasagna as well as originals such as penne with goat cheese and mushrooms or herb crusted fish. Save room for the mango cheesecake. *Dinner only. Closed September.*

Around Tortola

Calamaya (495-2126), at Maya Cove, East End, may look like a shack when it's not open but this is the spot for excellent casual dining overlooking the marina. Black fettucine with lobster, spaghetti with cilantro pesto, jerk chicken, and local seafood prepared in various West Indian styles are the house specialties. There's usually entertainment Wednesdays and Fridays. *Open for breakfast too, and open almost every day, including many holidays.*

Jolly Roger (495-4559) is at West End past the ferry dock. A full breakfast menu, plus pizzas, hamburgers, stewed and cracked conch, spicy rotis, and burgers are all specialties here and there's a Caribbean barbecue weekend nights. *Closed September.*

Paradise Club (495-4606), on Cane Garden Bay, serves sandwiches, ice cream, and great island drinks on an charming outdoor terrace with a superb view of the bay.

Eclipse (495-1646), at Penn's Landing, is the place to come for the most innovative cuisine in the British Virgin Islands. The international offerings draw on everything from Asian to fusion and there's also a trendy two-page grazing menu. It's all served in a casual outdoor setting with tables scattered across a terrace completely open to the tropical breezes. Head here Sundays for the tasty brunch, which is available from 11 am to 3 pm. *Closed Mondays. Dinner only, plus brunch only on Sunday.*

Sebastian's On the Beach (495-4212), on the north shore at Apple Bay, is a great place to come for breakfast (fresh fruit, eggs, pancakes) or lunch (hamburgers, sandwiches, grilled vegetables, and salads). The terrace overhangs the beach with superb views of pelicans diving for fish. Open for dinner also.

TORTOLA'S GREAT PUBS

They're scattered about Road Town. You'll find great selections of beers and ales, tasty portions of traditional pub fare, and dart boards.

Virgin Queen (494-2310) is the most popular pub on Tortola. Locals and the yachting crowd gather here for bangers and mash, shepherd's pie, fish and chips, and their famous Queen's Pizza. Naturally, the bar is stocked with a fine selection of stouts, ales, and lagers.

Pusser's Pub (494-3897) is almost always hopping. Come here for Pusser's Rum drinks and a selection of meat pies as well as burgers and pizzas. The young crowd heads here every Thursday for the famous "nickel beer night."

WHERE TO GO FOR GREAT LOCAL FOOD

Local sauces are usually spicy and full of onions, much like Creole sauces, and they are often served over fresh fish. Whelk and conch are seafood specialties. Local goat and mutton is common, and quite tasty, especially if it has been stewed for a while. Rotis, which originated in Trinidad, are common enough now to qualify as a local dish.

The Apple (495-4437), in Little Apple Bay, mixes continental cuisine with great local West Indian dishes. Come here for local snapper or conch with a spicy Creole sauce and the house specialty, whelk. Tablecloths, high-backed chairs, and candlelight make for a romantic setting. Lunch is casual and includes a tasty vegetarian roti.

The "Fish Fry" is on Zion Hill Road on the northwest end of Tortola. This is outdoors and doesn't have a name, but every Friday and Saturday evening locals stoke up the fires by the side of the road and cook excellent local fish here. It's across the street from the Apple Restaurant, a minute or so walk from Little Apple Bay on Tortola's North Shore.

Mrs. Scatliffe's (495-4556) is on Carrot Bay. Known as the Queen of local cooking, she serves family style meals in her home every evening. Menus change nightly, but might include curried goat, pot roast pork, chicken and coconut, and conch fritters. She serves lunch, too, Monday through Friday. *Reservations are necessary for dinner.*

Roti Palace (494-4196), in Road Town, serves up some of the best rotis on the island in this sparsely furnished spot. Rotis are curries wrapped in flat bread. Choose from goat, whelk, conch, beef, or chicken (you'll want the boneless). Be sure to try the delicious homemade mango chutney. *Lunch only.*

Struggling Man's (494-4163) is a waterfront spot on Sea Cow's Bay on Tortola's south shore. Come here for curried mutton, stewed conch and fish, and rotis. There's no extra charge for the great views of neighboring islands.

Quito's Gazebo (495-4837) is on Cane Garden Bay and owned by local recording star Quito Rhymer. This is a good place to come for fresh local fish West Indian style, conch stew, or curried chicken. Every night but Monday and Wednesday you can also hear Quito performing live.

Virgin Queen (494-2310), in Road Town, is an incredibly popular pub that also serves great local dishes. Come here for salt fish, mutton stew, and peas and rice.

Beyond Tortola's East End
Pusser's Marina Cay (494-2174) has free ferry service (schedules page 124) from their dock on Beef Island to their restaurant on Marina Cay. The dinner menu features barbecue ribs, grilled steak, lobster, and fresh fish served in their al fresco beachside restaurant.

The Last Resort (495-2520) is actually on a tiny little islet just off Beef Island. Not only is there a buffet of roast beef and Yorkshire Pudding plus a huge array of other choices, there's also Tony Snell's popular, after-dinner show.

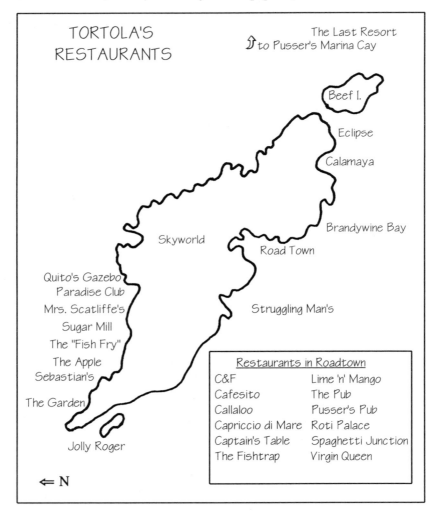

TORTOLA'S RESTAURANTS

The Last Resort
to Pusser's Marina Cay

Beef I.

Eclipse

Calamaya

Brandywine Bay

Skyworld

Road Town

Quito's Gazebo
Paradise Club
Mrs. Scatliffe's
Sugar Mill
The "Fish Fry"
The Apple
Sebastian's

Struggling Man's

The Garden

Jolly Roger

⇐ N

Restaurants in Roadtown	
C&F	Lime 'n' Mango
Cafesito	The Pub
Callaloo	Pusser's Pub
Capriccio di Mare	Roti Palace
Captain's Table	Spaghetti Junction
The Fishtrap	Virgin Queen

TORTOLA'S GREAT BARS

FOR SUNSETS AND VIEWS AND CIVILIZED COCKTAILS

Treasure Isle Hotel
Garden Restaurant at Long Bay Beach Resort
Sugar Mill's Gazebo Lounge
Ft. Burt's expansive terrace
Skyworld

TO BE RIGHT WHERE IT'S HAPPENING

Pusser's Pub in Road Town
The Pub
Virgin Queen
Scoundrel's
Pusser's West End
Jolly Roger

GREAT BAREFOOT BARS

Bomba's Shack
All the bars along Cane Garden Bay
Sebastian's
Long Bay Resort's Beach Bar

NIGHTLIFE ON TORTOLA

On Friday and Saturday nights and Sunday afternoons many Tortola spots feature live entertainment. However, you can usually find live music any night of the week, especially on season. BVI musicians often play at a different hotel or bar each night, so if you find a group you particularly like, find out where they will be playing next.

Many musicians travel back and forth between the islands but no one beats guitarist Ruben Chinnery, who often entertains on several islands in the course of a single afternoon and evening.

One of the great things about all of this music is that generally you are listening to it outside, under the blanket of Caribbean stars! Remember, bands do move around, so it's best to call the establishment to see which band will be there or to check the Limin' Times*, which comes out weekly, for up-to-the-minute schedules of who is playing where.*

Love Songs
For romantic sounds, be sure to find wonderful Ruben Chinnery, who hails from Jost Van Dyke and who plays the acoustic guitar and sings ballads and love songs. Or check out Quito, who plays love songs at his own restaurant, Quito's Gazebo.

Steel Bands
Do catch a steel band at least once — the music is quite beautiful and it's hard to believe these smooth mellow sounds are made by striking oil drums. This form of music originated in Trinidad but is now found all over the Caribbean. Great BVI steel bands include Pan-Vibes and the Shooting Stars.

Fungi Bands
Fungi bands are a type of scratch band that combines flutes with washboards, bottles, gourds, and other household items. It's hard not to get caught up in the fun and rhythm of a fungi band! See if you can find the fungi bands Spark Plugs or Romeo and the Injectors.

Reggae
O-2 and Blue Haze play a kind of modernized Reggae plus contempory top-40s and rock and roll — all great for shaking-it-up or dancing cheek-to-cheek.

LIVE ENTERTAINMENT ON TORTOLA

Bomba's Shack. Local bands like "Blue Haze" and "O-2" play here Wednesday evenings and Sunday afternoons and at his famous all-night Full Moon Parties. *Apple Bay, North Shore, 495-4148.*

Jolly Roger. Live music by local bands and bands from the states entertain every Friday and Saturday (and sometimes Thursday). *West End, 495-4559.*

Long Bay Beach Resort. There's a live band on Tuesday and Friday nights. Tuesday it's usually the steel band Pan-Vibes and Friday the fungi band Spark Plugs. *Long Bay, North Shore, 495-4252.*

Myett's. Friday, Saturday, Sunday, and Monday nights local bands keep this popular spot hopping. *Cane Garden Bay, 495-9649.*

Old Mill. This place, on the top floor of the old mill, often has music but it's forever opening and closing. Check it out on Wickham's Cay I. *Road Town.*

The Pub. Ruben Chinnery entertains here on Friday evenings and there's often dance music late Friday and Saturday on-season. *Road Town, 494-2608.*

Pusser's Landing. Local bands make appearances Friday and Saturday nights. Sunday afternoons there is sometimes a steel band. *Frenchman's Cay, West End, 495-4554.*

Quito's Gazebo. Recording star Quito Rhymer plays guitar and sings his love songs and ballads every night but Monday and Wednesday. There are also local bands here on weekends. *Cane Garden Bay, North Shore, 495-4837.*

Sebastian's. Frequently a local band plays here on weekends. Often, Saturday night it's the steel band Pan-Vibes and Sunday it's the fungi band The Spark Plugs. *Apple Bay, North Shore, 495-4212.*

BOMBA'S SHACK

Most everybody has heard of Bomba by now. His Full Moon Parties are famous throughout the Caribbean. Drive by the place during the day and you might mistake it for a junk pile, but Wednesdays, Sundays, and full moon nights the place, and the beach and fields around it, are packed. You can stop here any day any time after 10 am and try Bomba's specialty, a blend of passionfruit, guava, banana, papaya, pineapple, and orange juices mixed with Bomba's homemade rum — a secret recipe handed down by his family.

DON'T MISS

Dinner at Brandywine Bay Restaurant

Sunset cocktails on Ft. Burt's terrace -- you can watch the lights of Road Town appear all around the Harbour

A visit to at least one Pusser's store

Ice cream at the little stand called Chad's in Road Town

At least one snorkel, anywhere

Browsing through one (or all) of the Sea Urchin shops for great swimwear, casual clothing, sandals, and souvenirs

The view from Skyworld

A cappuccino or a Mango Bellini or a bowl of penne with spicy tomato sauce at Capriccio di Mare in Road Town

Taking at least one nautical adventure, from renting a dinghy to going on a day sail

Breakfast at Sebastian's, watching the pelicans dive bomb for their morning repast

Dinner at Long Bay's elegant Garden Restaurant

TORTOLA'S GREAT RESORTS AND INNS

Bear in mind that BVI resorts are in scale with the islands and quite small compared to those in the U.S. A full-service resort in the U.S. might have 800 rooms and, in fact, there are only about 870 rooms in all of the British Virgin Islands! Also, in the BVI, as on most islands, many "expected" services such as room service or dry cleaning usually aren't available (there is only one dry cleaner in the BVI). The trade-off for this lack of "services" is an extraordinary peace and quiet, an incredibly relaxed pace, and truly empty beaches.

*Rates are **per night for two people** without meals on season, and do not include service charge (usually 10%) and 7% Government tax. Ranges reflect range of accommodations. Off-season rates are in parentheses.*

LONG BAY BEACH RESORT & VILLAS

A spectacular mile-long beach, two pools, tennis courts, two appealing restaurants, and great accommodations make this resort a spot you never have to leave, but it's also a great location if you want to explore — it's easy to go to Smuggler's Cove or West End or hop over to Jost Van Dyke.

Tucked behind the sea grape trees along the beach are cozy rooms on stilts (some with ocean views) and also spacious deluxe units with large balconies and walk-in showers. Sea grapes are between these deluxe units and the beach and the second-floor units have better views. Scattered up the hillside are studios with jacuzzis, poolside studios, and one-, two-, and three-bedroom villas with full kitchens. The hillside is steep and views from most of the hillside units are stunning (and the walk back and forth from the beach or dinner is superb exercise). Units have air-conditioned bedrooms, phones, coffee makers, and refrigerators. Most have TVs.

The Garden Restaurant is an excellent spot for dinner and the casual Beach Restaurant is open all day (and every evening on season). There are two swimming pools, an extremely informal 9-hole "pitch and putt" golf course, three tennis courts, a delightful boutique, and a little commissary. *115 units. Rates: $300-$395 ($180-$210), villas more. General Manager: Bernd Gable. Reservations: 800-729-9599. Tel: 284-495-4252. Fax 284-495-4677. P.O.Box 433. E-mail: reservations@longbay.com.*

PUSSER'S FORT BURT HOTEL

If you want to be right at the edge of Road Town in an historic inn with great views of the harbour and a good restaurant on site, this is the place.

Fort Burt is one of Tortola's best preserved historical sites. In the 17th century the Dutch built a fort here, perched on a hill at the edge of Road Town harbour, an excellent location for spotting the approach of enemy ships. Today it offers stunning views of the harbour, Sir Francis Drake Channel, and neighboring islands. A steep driveway leads up to the base of the fort. Units vary in size from very small to spacious, but all have balconies and two have their own private circular outdoor pools, perfect for daytime sunning and nighttime stargazing. All rooms are air-conditioned and have fridges and fax machines.

The open-air restaurant is an elegant setting for all meals. There's a small indoor bar, a comfortable lounge with leather sofas, a shaded terrace for reading or sharing a libation, and a swimming pool for guests. Road Town is a short walk away. The staff can arrange island tours, trips to the beach, and sailing and snorkeling excursions. *19 units. Rates: $99-$255 ($75-$225), two-bedroom suite $370 ($295). General Manager: Glendora Jones. Tel: 284-494-2587. Fax: 284-494-2002. P.O. Box 3380. E-mail: fortburt@pussers.com.*

THE SUGAR MILL

Stay here when you want a simple yet sophisticated hideaway with a little patch of beach and an excellent restaurant. You can spend your days reading and resting or use it as a cozy base from which to explore.

Comfortable rooms, cooled by ceiling fans and air conditioning, spill down the hillside at this intimate north shore spot. Each has a little kitchen with a fridge and microwave and private balconies look out to the ocean through the trees. A 360-year old sugar mill with handsome stone walls provides the appealing setting for reception, casual breakfasts, a little bar, and fine dining in the well-known Sugar Mill restaurant, open for dinner only and one of the best on the island (see page 78). Islands, a little beach grill, serves burgers, salads, and West Indian dishes for lunch and, Tuesday through Saturday from January through April, also offers West Indian-inspired dinner items.

The petite beach across the street is calm and good for swimming and snorkeling (there's a reef right at the end). Because it's tiny it's private, as non-guests rarely stop here. You can also take a dip in the circular pool. *Closed August, September. 24 units, including 2 villas. Rates: $185-620 ($150-$500). General Manager: Patrick Conway. Reservations: 800-462-8834. Tel: 284-495-4355. Fax: 284-495-4696. P.O. Box 425. E-mail: sugmill@surfbvi.com.*

VILLAS OF FORT RECOVERY ESTATES

Pamelah Jacobson makes this cozy spot what it is — a great place to chill out, cool down, and simply recover from the stresses of stateside life.

Right on a smallish beach five minutes from West End by car is this very casual resort that looks out toward Frenchman's Cay and St. John in the USVI. You drive through a gate and slip into a private and relaxing world full of brilliant tropical flowers. There is one lovely three-bedroom villa here but, despite the name, the other accommodations are more like comfortable apartments on two floors. One- and two-bedroom units are staggered so that balconies are fairly private. Interiors are bright and designed to be easy to live in, with small but full kitchens and separate living areas. Penthouse units (second floor units) have high ceilings and an airy feel. There are TVs and VCRs and videos are available for rent. Rates include a continental breakfast with delicious homemade breads.

Although there is no restaurant, dinner can be served to you in your living room or on your terrace. And, in fact, one dinner is free for each week you stay there. The beach is smallish but very calm and good for swimming and snorkeling and there is also a swimming pool. Water sports, boat trips, yoga, and massage therapy are available. *17 units. Rates for one-bedroom units: $230-$260 ($145-$165). General Manager: Pamelah Jills Jacobson. Reservations: 800-367-8455. Tel: 284-495-4354. Fax: 284-495-4036. P.O. Box 239. E-mail: villas@fortrecovery.com.*

OTHER GOOD CHOICES

PUSSER'S LAMBERT BEACH RESORT

Colorfully-decorated rooms and suites look out to gardens or to beautiful Elizabeth Beach on Tortola's somewhat remote northeast shore. There's a charming, open-air restaurant, swimming pool, and tennis court. *38 rooms and suites. Rates: $140-$320 (off-season $100-260). General Manager: Pia Piccoli. Reservations: 800-225-4255. Tel: 284-495-2877. Fax 284-495-2876. www.pussers.com*

THE OLE WORKS INN

The location on Cane Garden Bay is the draw here. Rooms are modest but Tortola's most famous beach is right across the street and can be your playground day and night. The main building is a 300-year old restored sugar factory. Some units look out to the beach and others into the hills. There is also a simple honeymoon tower. *18 units. Rates: $140-$265 ($60-$175). Proprietor: Quito Rhymer. Tel: 284-495-4837. Fax 284-495-9618. P.O. Box 560.*

TAMARIND CLUB HOTEL
Located a little less than a mile inland from remote Josiah's Bay Beach is this quiet hideaway. Rooms are clustered together and are cozy but comfortable and some face the appealing pool with its swim-up bar. Some rooms are air-conditioned. The inspired dinner menu changes nightly but includes many choices each night, such as an excellent black bean soup, spicy chili, chargrilled mahi mahi, West Indian ribs, or grilled filet. *9 rooms. Room rates, including continental breakfast: $100-$180 ($75-$125). General Manager: Dawn Rosenberg. Tel: 284-495-2477. Fax 284-495-2795. P.O. Box 509. E-mail: tamarindclub.com*

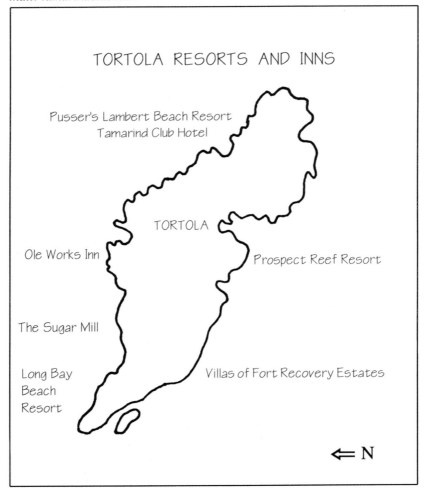

MORE THINGS PEOPLE USUALLY WISH THEY HAD KNOWN SOONER

❑September is exceptionally slow and some resorts and restaurants close up. Some stay closed through mid-October. Tortola is the least shut-down island (only a handful of restaurants and resorts actually close) but Virgin Gorda is exceptionally quiet during this time and almost nothing is open on Jost Van Dyke. The advantage of traveling this time of year is that you have the beaches and roads to yourself.

❑When you fly from Puerto Rico to the BVI you are almost always over islands and you really get to see how close everything is. If you are flying on American Eagle, generally the best views are out of the right side of the plane (and the left side going home). You'll get a sense of how these politically separated islands are actually one long string of hills poking out of the sea.

❑You'll see goats, cows, roosters, horses, and an occasional pig on roads and also in town. Contrary to popular opinion, roosters not only crow at dawn but whenever they bloody well feel like it, which is why some people prefer air conditioning despite the beautiful breezes.

❑Jost Van Dyke is more crowded on weekends because day-trippers come from St. Thomas.

❑To the delight of taxi drivers and the dismay of almost everyone else, from November to April cruise ships disgorge passengers several days a week and they spill into Road Town, Sage Mountain, Skyworld, and Cane Garden Bay. (Check the paper for cruise ship schedules if you want to avoid these crowds).

MORE
DRIVING HINTS

ROUND-A-BOUTS

Round-a-bouts are places where four or five roads run into a circle. The driver enters the circle, drives along part of it, and then exits on the road of choice. The only people who go full circle are those who want to go back the way they came or those who've spent their lives going around in circles. Remember to turn left into the circle, and left out of the circle. And to drive clockwise when you are in the circle.

BEWARE THE MULE

There is sometimes a mule tied to a tree on the dirt road that lies between BVI Boardsailing and De Loose Mongoose on Trellis Bay. On occasion, he tangles his rope around the trees on one side of the road and then heads over to the other side of the road to munch on tree leaves. Sometimes the rope becomes tightly stretched across the road about three feet above the ground, successfully halting all traffic. If this happens to you and you happen to be the only car in sight, hop out of whatever side of the car he's not on (mules have big teeth and like to bite) and give the rope a good tug. You should be able to get enough slack to get the rope to the ground so you can drive across it. Or you can always head back to DeLoose Mongoose and have another beer.

ROAD SIGNS

Although road signs have been posted in town and around the island, they are almost as unfamiliar to the residents as they are to you. For years, locals have used landmarks for directions so it really helps to know that in Road Town everything is near the Chase Bank or the round-a-bout or Bobby's supermarket and around the island places are always near a bay (Sea Cow's or Long or Apple and so on).

11. VIRGIN GORDA

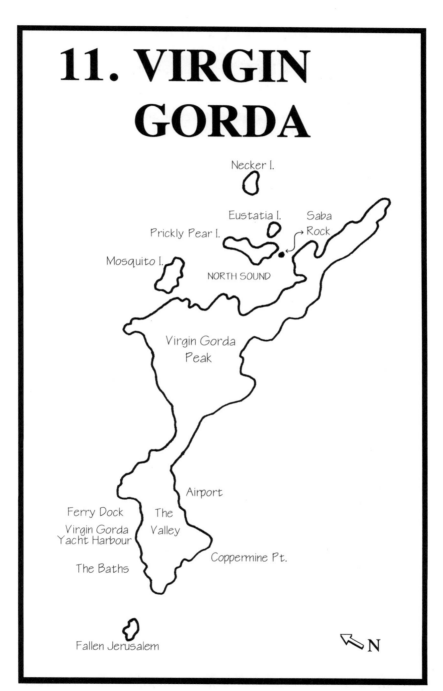

Necker I.

Eustatia I.   Saba
Prickly Pear I.   Rock
Mosquito I.
                  NORTH SOUND

Virgin Gorda
Peak

Airport

Ferry Dock   The
Virgin Gorda   Valley
Yacht Harbour

                  Coppermine Pt.
The Baths

Fallen Jerusalem   N

VIRGIN GORDA
IN A NUTSHELL

Virgin Gorda is a ten mile long island that lies east of Tortola. Only 2,894 people live there, but it's the second most populated British Virgin Island. The southern and northern ends of Virgin Gorda are somewhat isolated from each other and visiting these two areas of Virgin Gorda are completely different experiences.

The southern end of Virgin Gorda, which is rather flat and strewn with giant boulders, is referred to as The Valley or Spanish Town. The famous Baths are here, as are several other small but popular beaches. You'll also find a handful of restaurants and bars and, at the Virgin Gorda Yacht Harbour, a cluster of shops.

This part of Virgin Gorda is fairly compact, with beaches, shops, restaurants, and places to stay all within a few easy minutes of each other. When you want to go anywhere, you walk or drive or taxi across land, the way you do on most islands.

The middle section of Virgin Gorda is one big mountain, the top of which is a National Forest. Several very lovely, frequently deserted beaches are strung along the western shore here. A single road runs up over this steep mountain, connecting the Valley and North Sound.

The long, northern shore of Virgin Gorda, along with the shores of Mosquito and Prickly Pear Islands, almost completely encircles the remarkable North Sound, one of the world's most protected sounds.

Resorts are scattered around the rim of North Sound. With one exception, these resorts are only accessible by boat. When you visit the northern end of Virgin Gorda, instead of going by land you go by sea. Restaurants, stores, and resorts are scattered along the shore but are not connected by roads. To get anywhere, you travel back and forth across water, via water taxi or your own little boat.

PART 1: THE VALLEY

Note: This chapter on Virgin Gorda is divided into two sections: The Valley, which begins here, and North Sound, which begins on page 108.

WHAT YOU CAN DO IN THE VALLEY

You can visit the Virgin Gorda Yacht Harbour which has several restaurants, shops, a bank, and the Virgin Gorda office of the BVI Tourist Board. This area may look little to you, but it's the largest "town" on the island! You can also swim at The Baths, hike to several other beaches, and go see Coppermine Point, a ruin of a copper mine on a windswept rocky point.

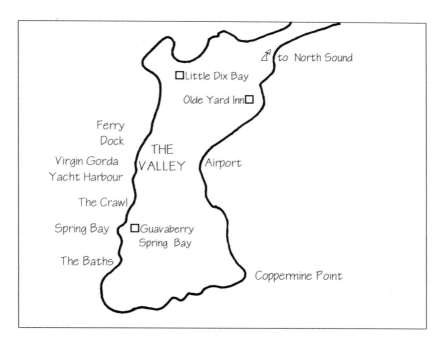

GETTING TO THE VALLEY

You can get here by public ferry from Road Town or West End on Tortola, or Charlotte Amalie on St. Thomas (see Appendix for Ferry Schedules). Or you can fly here from Tortola, St. Thomas, or San Juan. If you are on Virgin Gorda's North Sound, you will need to go to Leverick Bay or Gun Creek and then drive or catch a taxi.

EXPLORING THE VALLEY

The Virgin Gorda Yacht Harbour is the "hub" of The Valley. The whole southern end of Virgin Gorda is strewn with giant, smooth-sided boulders. At The Baths, which are probably Virgin Gorda's most famous landmark, these giant boulders are scattered in the water creating dramatic pools and grottoes.

The Baths, the other beaches in The Valley, the trails, the snorkeling areas, and Coppermine Point are all part of the BVI National Parks Trust, a system of protected water and land areas. Please respect signs and don't leave anything behind but your footprints.

RENTING A CAR OR HIRING A TAXI

You can rent a car or jeep for $50-$60 a day from **L & S Jeep Rental** (495-5297), **Mahogany Car Rentals** (495-5469), or **Speedy's** (495-5240). They'll pick you up at the Virgin Gorda Yacht Harbour or the airport if you like.

You can get a taxi at the airport or at the Taxi Stand in the parking lot south of the Yacht Harbour or call **L & S Taxi** (495-5297) or **Speedy's** (495-5240) or **Mahogany Taxi** (495-5469) and they'll send a taxi right over. Taxis vary from brightly-striped, canopied, open "safari buses" to jeep-type vehicles to regular sedans. The fare to anywhere from anywhere in the Valley is $2 to $3 per person. Drivers are happy to drop you at the beach and pick you up later. It's $20 for up to four people to Gun Creek or Leverick Bay. An hour and a half island tour is $30 for two people.

SHORTCUT FROM THE FERRIES
TO THE YACHT HARBOUR

Public ferries arrive just north of the Virgin Gorda Yacht Harbour. Taxis meet the ferries and friendly drivers will take you anywhere. If you want to see the Yacht Harbour first, you can easily walk if you know the shortcut. Look for the small building on your right. Just past it, turn right and head toward the large field bordered by a chain-link fence (don't worry, it's public property). You'll see a path that leads to an opening in the fence. Follow it and in a minute or two you'll be right at Yacht Harbour.

VIRGIN GORDA YACHT HARBOUR

Here you will find a marina and a charming shopping complex built around a courtyard. This is also the home of the well-known Bath & Turtle Restaurant and Pub. Look for signs for the BVI Tourist Board which is on the outside of the complex, facing the water. You can stop here for maps, brochures, and menus, and they'll be glad to answer any of your questions.

Island Happenings: Check out the bulletin board in the middle of the parking lot. You'll find printed and handwritten notices of events, band appearances, restaurant menus, schedule changes, and other information.

VIRGIN GORDA YACHT HARBOUR SHOPPING

Buck's Food Market (495-5423) carries fresh, canned, and frozen foods.

The Commissary (495-5555), owned by Little Dix Resort, offers groceries, fresh produce, gourmet items, and excellent sandwiches, salads, breads and pastries prepared by Little Dix chefs. You'll also find gift items and t-shirts.

DIVE BVI (495-5513) has great t-shirts, sunglasses, books, and sportswear as well as diving and snorkel equipment (including on-the-spot prescription masks). They also offer dives and instruction for all ability levels.

Kaunda's Tropix (495-5636) is the place to come for a great selection of local music tapes. Also, you can bring your film here for quick processing. They pierce ears, too!

Margo's Jewelry Boutique (495-5237) showcases handcrafted gold and silver pieces of jewelry and carved wood sculptures.

Island Drug Centre (495-5449) is a good source for prescriptions.

Pelican Pouch Boutique (495-5599) has some of the best women's bathing suits, beach cover-ups, hats, and beach bags in the BVI.

Scoops (no phone) features colorful sun dresses and island sportswear.

Virgin Gorda Craft Shop (495-5137) carries wonderful locally-made items.

Wine Cellar and Bakery (495-5250) carries oven-fresh French bread plus pastries, cookies, sodas, wines, and bottled liquor. On season you can get excellent sandwiches here.

DRIVING TO THE BATHS, SOME BEACHES, AND SOME OTHER GREAT STOPS

In The Valley you can visit Coppermine Point, an old mine on a rocky, rugged point. You can also visit The Baths and other nearby beaches. In addition, you can drive to several deserted beaches just north of The Valley. These directions all begin at the Virgin Gorda Yacht Harbour.

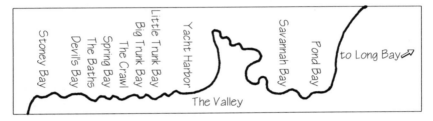

TO COPPERMINE POINT

Turn right out of the Yacht Harbour parking lot. In a little under a mile the road curves abruptly left. After this curve, look for the first road on your left and turn onto it. Follow this road until it ends at a "T." Turn right and stay on this road until it ends. The road can be rutted and very bouncy and you may feel that you are lost, but, in about ten minutes you will get to a rocky point with an old mine shaft and a great view of crashing waves.

TO REACH SPRING BAY, THE CRAWL, THE BATHS, AND DEVIL'S BAY

Turn right out of the Yacht Harbour parking lot. In a little under a mile from the Yacht Harbour, the road turns sharply left and then straightens out. Just stay on this main road. By the way, the hills you see in the distance are not part of Virgin Gorda but are actually the hills of Ginger and Salt Islands.

To reach **Spring Bay** and **The Crawl**, watch for the sign on the right about a mile and a half from the Yacht Harbour. Turn off at the sign, follow the road to the end, and park. **Spring Bay**, which has a pretty beach, is down a little path. **The Crawl**, a natural pool formed by rocks, is great for novice snorkelers. You can get to it by following the marked path.

To reach **The Baths**, keep going straight on the main road until it ends in a circle about two miles from the Yacht Harbour. When you see the **Mad Dog** restaurant on your right, you're just about there. Park your car anywhere along the side of the circle. You'll see a restaurant called Top of the Baths and some shops. Information about this section of National Park is posted in the little gazebo. At the circle you have the choice of walking to **The Baths** (350 yards and ten minutes) or **Devil's Bay** (600 yards and fifteen minutes). A map at the gazebo shows how these two trails connect. Devil's Bay is usually less crowded than very popular The Baths.

The path to The Baths is clearly etched into the ground and drops gently, curving around the giant boulders, which, along with trees, provide plenty of shade. At the beach, you'll find the **Poor Man's Bar**, a good stop for cold drinks, cold beer, hot dogs, and other snacks.

DRIVING TO SAVANNAH BAY BEACH AND POND BAY BEACH FROM THE VALLEY

Savannah Bay Beach and Pond Bay Beach are really easy to reach. They are only about ten minutes from the Virgin Gorda Yacht Harbour but still often deserted.

From the Virgin Gorda Yacht Harbour parking lot, turn left onto the main road (remembering to keep to the left). By the way, those round steel bars you occasionally drive over are to keep the goats out. When the road "T's" turn right and stay on the main road. It will curve left and then you'll pass the Olde Yard Inn and go over a hill and you'll suddenly see lovely beaches ahead of you on the left.

To get to **Savannah Bay**, which is the first beach on your left, look for a turn-off on the left just when the road flattens out. It's not easy to spot since the brush comes right to the road. Drive in and park. **Pond Bay Beach** is a little farther along this same road. Take the left at the sign to Mango and Paradise Beach Resorts, look for a parking place, and walk down to the beach.

TO REACH DESERTED LONG BAY BEACH

This beach is usually deserted. The shoreline is long, occasionally giving way momentarily to trees and scrubby shrubs. A boat or two may be anchored at the far end. The water is generally very calm here and there is fine swimming and reefs nearby for snorkeling. The sand can be full of bits and pieces of weatherworn coral.

Time: It's a twenty minute drive from the Virgin Gorda Yacht Harbour parking lot.

Follow the directions to Pond Bay and take the left turn-off to Paradise Beach and Mango Bay. This is a fairly bumpy dirt road but it turns into concrete in those occasional places where it gets quite steep. The only turn-offs are either private driveways or lead to one of several little condo resorts. Just stick to the road and eventually you'll end up at Long Bay Beach.

When you are very near the entrance to Mango Beach Resort, the view off to the left looks like one large island in the distance, but actually it's quite a few. From south to north, it is Beef, Tortola, Scrub, and then Great Camanoe. The much smaller, much closer little islands are the Dogs. From here you can see Great Dog and George Dog. In a moment West and East Seal Dogs will appear.

After you go over a hill and pass the Diamond Beach Club on your left, you'll suddenly drop right to the edge of Long Bay Beach. There's a lot of nice sand and protected water.

"When you come to the fork in the road, take it."

— Yogi Berra

#
GREAT THINGS TO DO ON VIRGIN GORDA

Treat yourself to breakfast at the Olde Yard Inn. You may want to do this twice, so you can sample the superb French toast and the tasty island pancakes! Eggs are on the menu, too.

Go to the airport. Watch the little planes land on the tiny strip of dirt Virgin Gordans call a runway. Passengers get out of the planes looking startled, especially when they realize they've been part of the show!

Rent a dinghy and explore North Sound. You can spend the day putt-putting about or you can snorkel over the side or you can just drift about and take in the scenery.

Go floating. Get on one of those yellow or blue floats and just lie there. If you are into decadent snorkeling bring your mask, hang your head over the end, and gaze underwater. Otherwise just lie there and float. It's so relaxing.

Head to Biras Creek Resort for a sweeping sunset view over cocktails and an elegant dinner. Call ahead (494-3555) and they'll pick you up free at Gun Creek.

Walk around the Virgin Gorda Yacht Harbour. Take a look at all the sailboats and motor yachts.

Stop by the Mine Shaft Cafe at sunset time. You'll see one of the world's great views. Come back at night for a romantic, casual meal under the stars.

BOAT TRIPS AND BOAT RENTALS IN THE VALLEY

There are several great cruises available that will take you snorkeling or sightseeing. On a calm day it's also quite easy and a lot of fun to rent a little boat and go from the Virgin Gorda Yacht Harbour to The Baths and on to the other beaches along the western shores of Spanish Town.

CAPTAINED BOAT TRIPS FROM THE VALLEY

Let someone else do the driving and sit back and enjoy the remarkable views from the water when you take one of these cruises. Choose a sail boat or a powerboat and pick a planned itinerary or create your own!

Spirit of Anegada. Little Dix Bay (495-5555) offers daily sailing trips on a 49' sailboat, the *Spirit of Anegada*. The captain usually sails to uninhabited islands for some excellent snorkeling. A cold buffet luncheon is served on board. The cost is $95 per person (minimum 4 people, maximum 10). The *Spirit of Anegada* is also available for half-day trips for $60 per person including beverages or for private charter to almost anywhere for $650 a day or $400 a half-day, and can be chartered overnight or to a small cay for dinner.

Euphoric Cruises (494-5542) has a 28' Bertram powerboat that is available for day trips with a captain. The boat leaves from Virgin Gorda Yacht Harbour and will head to your choice of island(s), weather permitting. Cost is $675 for a full day; $450 a half day.

Sunset Cruise by Euphoric Cruises (494-5542) is a great sunset-cocktail cruise catered by Little Dix Resort. The boat is a 49' Albin Cruiser and it goes every Sunday and Wednesday. Although the exact route depends on the time of year and where the sun is setting, the captain usually heads up the west side of Virgin Gorda, turns into North Sound at Anguilla Point, and heads out of North Sound past Mosquito Island. The boat leaves Virgin Gorda Yacht Harbour at 4 pm and returns about 6:30 pm. There are usually about 20 people. Cost is $35 per person. A private charter is $800 a day, $475 a half day.

RENTING YOUR OWN LITTLE BOAT

Power Boat Rentals, Ltd. (494-5542). At Virgin Gorda Yacht Harbour, Ash Harrigan offers 24' Robolos. All rental boats come with biminis, vhf radio, stepladder, and anchor. Rates are $250 per day. Call for weekly rates. They'll deliver boats to (or pick you up in) Road Town, Trellis Bay, or Virgin Gorda.

HIKING, FITNESS, AND MINIATURE GOLF IN THE VALLEY

The BVI National Parks Trust maintains many parks and protected areas throughout the BVI, including The Baths, the beaches to the north and south of The Baths, and Gorda Peak National Park. There are trails and picnic spots.

Gorda Peak National Park. There is a south and north entrance to this 265-acre park, both accessible from the road between The Valley and North Sound. Signs and access are on the west side of the road. Here you will find fairly strenuous trails, a lookout tower, and picnic tables. The dense vegetation includes mahogany trees and orchids.

Devil's Bay and Stoney Bay. There are inland and coastal trails from The Baths to Devil's Bay, where you will find tranquil waters and good snorkeling. From Devil's Bay there is a trail to Stoney Bay.

Olde Yard Inn Fitness Center (495-5544). When you start feeling anxious about all those pina coladas you've been having for lunch, head over here for a real workout. There are bicycles, treadmills, free weights, and much more — all state of the art equipment, plus you can exercise while looking at a great view. Membership is available on a daily basis. Stay for a delicious lunch.

Miniature Golf at the Mine Shaft Cafe (495-5260). The view is great. For every hole-in-one, kids get a fruit punch but adults get a free "Cave In," the lethal specialty drink of the house. If you're good at this game you may regret it the next morning! *Fees are: $5 adults, $3 kids under 10 for 9 holes; $7 adults, $5 kids under 10 for 18 holes.*

> **"A much more effective and lasting method of facelifting than surgical technique is happy thinking, new interests and outdoor exercise."**
>
> *— Dr. Sara Murray Jordan*

THE VALLEY'S GREAT RESTAURANTS AND BARS

There are a number of excellent restaurants in Virgin Gorda's Valley area. Entrees at the two fine dining restaurants start around $17. Hamburgers, sandwiches, and salads at the casual restaurants are $6 to $10. All are open for lunch and dinner unless otherwise noted. And many of these places close or have a limited menu in September. Be sure also to check out the restaurant section for Virgin Gorda's North Sound (see page 113). You may not want to make the drive at night but you will find some wonderful lunchtime adventures.

FINE DINING IN THE VALLEY

Little Dix Resort (495-5555) serves exceptionally fine Continental cuisine in their Main Dining Room, which is actually an open-air "Pavilion" with a glorious view. Dinner here is a la carte, except for the lavish Monday night buffet. Breakfast and lunch are always buffets, and not really expensive, considering what you can have. At lunch there is an array of composed salads, cheeses, fresh fruits, breads, grilled fish, hot dogs and hamburgers, and a table of tempting sweets. If you want, you can skip all the hot and grilled items for a slightly lower price ($18 instead of $25). *Long pants and collared shirts required for men after sunset. Reservations necessary.*

Olde Yard Inn (495-5544) has a romantic restaurant which is open to the soft tropical breezes. Have a cocktail in the quiet bar and then enjoy everything from escargot to grilled super-fresh fish to tender veal sauteed with shrimp and wine to local lobster to their famous key lime pie, all served in an intimate atmosphere with taped, but extremely pleasant, classical music. Mondays and Friday nights in season a local guitarist entertains. Consider returning for a peaceful breakfast and enjoy great omelettes, pancakes, or the exceptional French toast. It's served from 7:30 to 10 am every day. *No lunch. No dinner Sundays. Usually closed for September. Reservations necessary for dinner.*

CASUAL DINING IN THE VALLEY

Bath & Turtle (495-5239), in the Yacht Harbour, is popular day and night, from early breakfasts to late evening snacks. Chili cheese dogs and pizza are house favorites here but you can get great sandwiches and salads. For dinner, you can also choose from selections such as grilled filet mignon, coconut fried shrimp, and lobster.

Chez Bamboo (495-5752), near the Yacht Harbour, blends Caribbean and French cuisine in a casual but romantic atmosphere. Conch gumbo, steak New Orleans, lobster, and pumpkin pecan pie are good choices. *Dinner only.*

Mad Dog (495-5830) is a great place to stop for hot dogs, BLTs, ice cold beer, and their real claim to fame, frozen Pina Coladas. It's tucked among sea grapes and boulders just before The Baths. *Lunch only.*

Giorgio's Table (495-5684), a short taxi ride north of the Valley, on Mahoe Bay, is the place to come for a romantic Italian lunch or dinner. Tables are on a little terrace set right at the water's edge.

Mine Shaft Cafe and Nightclub (495-5260) is perched atop a hill and shows off superb scenery. Views from the sunken bar and inside tables are awesome but the view from the deck is even better: brilliant sunsets and at night a billion stars and the lights of Tortola twinkling across the channel! Ribs, hamburgers, rotis, and caesar salad with grilled chicken are the house specialties.

Rock Cafe (495-5482) serves excellent Italian and Caribbean cuisine inside. Outside, La Tequila bar, set on a terrace sandwiched among the boulders, is the place to come for margaritas and Mexican appetizers. *Dinner only.*

Sip and Dip Grill (495-5544) at the Olde Yard Inn is an outdoor poolside grill and features refreshing gazpacho, Italian sausage with chili beans, char-grilled fish, pizza, grilled vegetables, and superb ice cream! Stop by Sunday evenings for the happening barbecue. *Lunch only, plus Sunday evening barbecue.*

NIGHTLIFE IN THE VALLEY

The Bath and Turtle. Crowds head here every Wednesday and Sunday nights to listen and dance to live local bands.

Chez Bamboo features jazz on Fridays and a live band on Sundays.

Little Dix Resort. On-season, every evening but Sunday there's entertainment.

Mine Shaft Cafe. This is the place to come for great full-moon parties.

Olde Yard Inn. Eldon John is on the guitar Monday and Friday evenings on season. Sunday nights there's a barbecue and a band.

Rock Cafe. Great local talent entertains here weekends.

105

THE VALLEY'S GREAT RESORTS AND INNS

In the Valley on Virgin Gorda you can choose a luxury resort, an intimate inn, comfortable cottages, or a fancy villa. Few places have rooms keys but you can lock yourself in at night, if you wish. To check out the resorts on Virgin Gorda's North Sound, see page 116.

*Rates are **per night for two people** on season (off-season in parentheses), without meals, and without 7% government tax or service charge (5%-15%).*

LITTLE DIX BAY

This luxury resort, now run by Rosewood, runs along the crescent-shaped shore of one of Virgin Gorda's calmest and prettiest bays.

Little Dix Bay is an upscale, elegant retreat. It's quiet and peaceful here. Despite the fact that this is one of the largest resorts in the BVI, you can feel wonderfully alone. Rooms, all with patios or balconies, are two or four to a building and scattered over a half-mile of beautifully-manicured grounds. Some have great views, and some are hidden among the trees, but all are spacious and handsomely furnished. King beds back up to stunning stone walls, beams run across the ceilings, and bathrooms are roomy with walk-in showers big enough for two. About half the rooms are air-conditioned. You will probably prefer these if outside noise bothers you.

The Pavilion restaurant, an open-air affair with an absolutely stunning view, is the setting for lavish buffet breakfasts and lunches and quiet and elegant a la carte dinners. The intimate Sugar Mill restaurant, al fresco and open on season, is nestled behind the inviting stone-walled bar. The casual Beach Grill serves sandwiches, salads, and grilled fish and steaks for lunch and dinner.

Head to the long silken beach for a peaceful walk, find yourself a yellow float and relax or look for turtles, snorkel (it's best at the northern edge of the beach), hike to Savannah Bay (just when you are sure you're lost in the woods, you'll suddenly be there), play tennis (there are seven courts, two lighted for night play), or have Little Dix drop you at a deserted beach with an elegant picnic. Children are welcome and most enjoy the superb children's program. There is a dress code here. *98 units, 4 suites. General Manager: Peter Shandlin. Rates: $550-$775 per night ($250-$425). Reservations: 800-928-3000. Tel: 284-495-5555. Fax 284-495-5661. P.O. Box 70. E-mail: www.rosewood-hotels.com.*

OLDE YARD INN

This is a remarkably relaxing little inn that you never have to leave but it's also a great base if you want to spend your days exploring Virgin Gorda.

You drive through a gateway into this appealing four-acre compound bright with tropical flowers. To the right is the open-air restaurant, the setting for elegant dinners and quiet breakfasts. Straight ahead, paths lead to cozy rooms, which are on two floors, all with small patios or balconies. Dark wood walls offer a respite from the sun and ceiling fans and louvered windows invite the breezes. Some rooms have air conditioning, coffee makers, and fridges, but none have phones or TVs. There is also a two-bedroom suite great for families.

To the left is an inviting library and a game room with all manner of board games plus a piano, TV, and VCR. Further left is the large and exceptionally lovely swimming pool with jetted spa. The Sip 'n Dip Grill is here, open for lunch and also the site of the Sunday night barbecues. Hidden behind the Grill is a state-of-the-art exercise room just in case you feel you've had one too many banana daiquiris. There's also a beauty salon.

Breakfast can be delivered to your room and free transportation is available to nearby, beautiful Savannah Bay Beach. The inn was awarded the CHA Green Hotelier of the Year Award. Management here goes out of their way here to make your stay extra special. *Usually closed September. 14 units, 1 two-bedroom suite. Rates: $195 ($110); suite $340 ($260). Proprietor: Carol Kaufman. Reservations: 800-653-9273. Tel: 284-495-5544. Fax 284-495-5968. P.O. Box 26. oldeyardinn.com.*

GUAVABERRY SPRING BAY VACATION HOMES

When you want to be on your own with a kitchen, whether you want a simple cottage or a fancy villa with a pool, check into Guavaberry.

Guavaberry's charming, hexagonally-shaped, wooden cottages are built on a little hill and hover at tree-top level. Many have great views of neighboring islands. One- and two-bedroom units have separate living/kitchen areas. Wide doors and louvered windows let in the breezes and show off the views (no air conditioning). A commissary carries essentials. It's a short walk to Spring Bay beach. Town, meaning the Yacht Harbour, is a mile north and the Baths are a mile south. You can also rent a range of private villas. *19 cottages, 15 villas. Rates: for a one-bedroom $175 ($120), two-bedroom $295 ($175), villas range from $240 ($163) per night to $6,600 ($4,400) a week. General Manager: Tina Goschler. Tel: 284-495-5227. Fax 284-495-5283. P.O. Box 20. E-mail: gsbhomes@surfbvi.com.*

PART 2: NORTH SOUND

North Sound is "paradise found" for water lovers. This water wonderland is the place to come for almost every possible kind of water sport. Here you can snorkel, swim, sail, windsurf, rent motorboats, and waterski, or you can learn how to do any of these things. There are also bars, casual eateries, and elegant restaurants.

GETTING TO NORTH SOUND

To get here from Tortola you can take the North Sound Express from Beef Island at the east end of Tortola which stops at Leverick Bay, Biras Creek, and Bitter End. (See Appendix for Ferry Schedules.) You can also drive or take a taxi to Leverick Bay or Gun Creek from the southern end of Virgin Gorda.

EXPLORING NORTH SOUND

In North Sound you travel mainly by water and you can take water taxis and ferries to restaurants and beaches. You can also rent your own dinghy and travel to many different beaches and unbelievably great snorkeling spots. If you are having lunch or dinner at Biras Creek or Drake's Anchorage, they will pick you up from Gun Creek or Leverick Bay. If you are having lunch, arrive early or stay late and enjoy the beach.

Water Taxis

You can hire a water taxi at the **Water Sports Center at Leverick Bay** (495-7366) to take you to Bitter End. The taxi will pick you up at Bitter End for the trip back any time you want before 5 pm. Round trip fare is $25.

Ferries

Free ferries run between Gun Creek and The Bitter End Yacht Club, and, as you will see on the next page, there are many boat trips that leave from The Bitter End. You can also walk from Bitter End to Biras Creek although the trail is a bit rough in spots. From Gun Creek, ferries run hourly on the half hour, from 6:30 am to 10:30 pm. From Bitter End, ferries run every hour on the hour, from 6 am to 11 pm.

EXPLORING NORTH SOUND BY DINGHY

North Sound is a great place to explore in a dinghy. There are beaches to go to, great snorkeling, very calm water to drift about in, restaurants to motor over to. For good snorkeling, head to Eustatia Sound, which is past Bitter End. For a quiet ride, putter in towards Deep Bay or around the outskirts of Eustatia Sound. Be careful and go slowly near Eustatia Sound Reef. The water gets pretty shallow and you don't want to run over any coral. If the water is calm you can go around Prickly Pear Island to two lovely beaches. For a drink or a snack, tie your boat up at the Sand Box restaurant dingy dock on Prickly Pear.

Where to rent dinghies.

The Bitter End Yacht Club (494-2746) rents Boston Whalers starting at $50 a half day. At **Leverick Bay**, Laura Barratt and Mike Foster run the **Water Sports Center** (495-7376) and rent 10' dinghies with 10 hp engines. Rates start at $60 a half-day, $75 a full day, including fuel. Snorkel equipment is $8 per day.

WATER SPORTS ON NORTH SOUND

There are two centers for water sports on North Sound: Leverick Bay and The Bitter End Yacht Club. You can rent all kinds of equipment.

Sailboards, Kayaks, Alden Rowing Shells, and Sail Boats

The Bitter End Yacht Club (494-2746) has a huge variety of water sports rentals. Come here to rent sailboards, sunfish, lasers, 19' Rhodes, J-24 sailboats, kayaks, Alden Rowing Shells and more. Rates are $15-$20 per hour.

The Water Sports Center at Leverick Bay (call Laura Barratt or Mike Foster, 495-7376) rents sunfish, Hobi Cats, and kayaks. Instruction is available in water-skiing, sunfishing, and Hobie Cat sailing for no additional charge.

Renting a powerboat

The Water Sports Center (495-7376) has a 24' center consol powerboat with bimini for rent for $280 a day plus fuel.

Parasailing

The Water Sports Center (495-7376) at Leverick Bay is the place to come for a thrilling ride for people age 2 to 92! You'll spot turtles and sea rays from 600' up. Rates are $55 for 10 minutes.

Water-skiing

The Water Sports Center (495-7376) at Leverick Bay offers water-skiing off of their competition mastercraft ski boat. Rates are $90 an hour, $60 a half hour. A barefoot bom is available for barefooters and a skylon pylon for those into wakeboarding.

GREAT BOAT AND SNORKELING TRIPS FROM NORTH SOUND

There are wonderful captained boat trips you can take from North Sound to various islands and to great snorkeling spots.

Statia Reef Snorkel Trip

Join one of the twice daily snorkel trips to beautiful Statia Reef on the 40' Ponce de Leon, a boat specially designed for snorkeling. The short morning trip, which makes one stop, is $5 per person. In the afternoon, there are three snorkeling stops for $10 per person. Call The Bitter End (494-2746).

Night Snorkeling
Take a guided night-snorkeling tour of Statia Reef led by the famous Kilbride group. Call The Bitter End (494-2746). This is offered in the summer only.

Powerboat to Anegada
Ride in comfort on the diesel-powered 50' Prince of Wales to Anegada. On Wednesdays you get a chance to explore the island, go to the beach, snorkel, and have lunch at Neptune's Treasure. The Friday trip is a full day at Loblolly Bay, beaching and snorkeling. The boat leaves at 9:30 and returns about 5:30. The price is $55 per person, including lunch. Call The Bitter End (494-2746).

Cigarette boat to Anegada or around the BVI
The Water Sports Center at Leverick Bay (495-7376) usually offers full day trips to Anegada on a speedy 33' cigarette boat. You go to Loblolly Bay or Cow Wreck Beach and have lunch at the Anegada Reef Hotel. The trip costs $600, 10 people maximum. You can also have a water tour of the BVI for $800.

Starlight Cruise
Cruise around North Sound under the stars while sipping champagne. The boat leaves at 6 pm and returns about 7:30 pm, sometimes with a steel band. Cost is $15 per person. Make reservations with The Bitter End (494-2746).

Ultimate Beaches
Sit back and relax and let a captain take you to one of many secluded beaches on a 26' speedboat. Or go to them all! It's your choice. Rates for two people are $375 per day, $200 a half day. Call The Bitter End Yacht Club (494-2746).

Deep Sea Fishing
The Bitter End (494-2746) runs half day offshore fishing trips on a 26' speedboat. Rates are $375 per day and $200 for a half day.

Sailing to Other Islands
Spice (495-7044) or book through Leverick Bay Watersports (495-7376), combines great snorkeling with outstanding sailing. This 51' sloop is perfect for a full or half-day of exploring the BVI waters. Cruise to the Baths, Cooper Island, the Dogs, Norman Island, Anegada, or even Jost Van Dyke. Experience extraordinary snorkeling and visit cool little beach bars. Every Thursday the *Spice* heads to Anegada for the day. Full days are $85 and half days are $55 per person. A private charter is $600 (maximum of 8).

111

'ING IN NORTH SOUND

LEVERICK BAY
Buck's Food Market (495-7372) carries groceries, fresh produce, liquor and beer, canned goods, and snacks.

Dive BVI (495-7328) sells a variety of swimwear, beachwear, postcards, colorful t-shirts, and island books, and also rents and sells snorkeling and diving equipment. First-rate instructors give lessons to all ability levels and there are many dive trips scheduled.

Palm Tree Gallery (495-7479) features a lovely selection of jewelry and local artwork, great books, postcards, fascinating games, gifts, and more. This place is definitely worth a stop (it's in the back of the plaza, past DIVE BVI).

Pusser's Company Store (495-7369) has a large collection of fashionable but comfortable clothing for the whole family plus all sizes of bottles of their famous rum, as well as souvenirs, postcards, and books.

NORTH SOUND RESORTS
Biras Creek and **Drake's Anchorage** have boutiques with a wide variety of fashionable sportswear, books, sunglasses, and sundries. At The Bitter End Yacht Club you'll find the Bitter End Emporium, with freshly baked breads and pastries, gourmet items, and canned goods, and Captain B's Trading Post with books, postcards, and souvenirs, and the Reeftique boutique.

A WORD OR TWO ABOUT SHOPPING IN THE BVI

You'll notice that the British Virgin Islands don't have the concentrated shopping areas devoted to tourists that you find on so many other islands. You also won't find the chain stores that appear on island after island, all offering similar merchandise.

What you will find instead are uncrowded little shops with lots of neat, original items. In the BVI you really can find things you can't find anywhere else.

NORTH SOUND'S GREAT RESTAURANTS AND BARS

All of these places are easily reachable by boat. If you are staying in North Sound you can dinghy from your resort to any of them for lunch. If you happen to be coming from the Valley for lunch or dinner, you can drive directly to Leverick Bay or Gun Creek. If you want to dine at Bitter End, catch the free ferry from Gun Creek. If you want to dine at Biras Creek, call ahead and they will send a boat to Gun Creek to pick you up. If you want to dine at Drake's Anchorage, call ahead and they will send a boat to pick you up at Leverick Bay.

Biras Creek Resort (495-3555) serves dinner in the "Castle," a stunning stonework structure set on a hill and overlooking both the Caribbean Sea and the calm North Sound. The expansive terrace and al fresco lounge is a romantic setting for an evening cocktail. Dinner is elegant and served by candlelight in several open air dining rooms. The sophisticated four-course menu changes nightly but each night it includes such choices as chargrilled wahoo, tenderloin of veal with capers and mustard, beef filet with a spicy tomato onion sauce, and a vegetarian entree. The cuisine and service here are outstanding and the setting is truly one of the very best in the BVI. This is a spot to have a splendid dinner, and then linger over Biras Creek's signature offering of port and Stilton. The wine list here is exceptional. Light salads, soups, sandwiches, and superb ice cream are served for the three-course lunch. Saturday the lunch choices are Italian (the spinach gnocchi are great). Mondays, Wednesdays, and Fridays a buffet lunch is served at the beach. Four-course dinners run $42-$58. *Dress is casual elegant (long trousers and collared shirts for men). Reservations for dinner essential.*

Captain Poncho's (no phone), within walking distance from the Gun Creek dock (on a hill to the left, after leaving the parking lot), is a popular local spot with a comfortable veranda open to the breezes. Hamburgers and sandwiches are offered for lunch and West Indian specialties are the dinner fare.

The Clubhouse at **The Bitter End Yacht Club** (494-2746) serves casual meals in an open-air dining room. Breakfast, for $13, includes a buffet plus a choice of eggs, pancakes, or french toast. Lunch is $17 and includes a buffet of salads, plus a choice of entrees such as a hamburger, chef salad, or conch fritters. Dinner, for $35, includes a salad and dessert buffet plus a choice of entrees including ribs, steaks, fish, or lobster (for a surcharge).

Drake's Anchorage Resort (494-2254) serves lunches and dinners right at the water's edge and it's quite a romantic experience, especially if you get a table close to the water. At night dine on fresh lobster, steak au poivre, grilled local swordfish, and boneless duck l'Orange. Save room for the chocolate mousse. If you are dining, Drake's will pick you up and take you back for free from Leverick Bay, Gun Creek, Bitter End, and Biras Creek. Entrees begin at $26. Call in the morning to arrange a lunch pick-up. For dinner, please make reservations by 3:30 pm. *Reservations for dinner essential.*

Last Stop Bar, up a little incline just across from the Gun Creek dock and overlooking the water, serves beverages all day long.

Pusser's Leverick Bay (4955-7370) has two restaurants overlooking North Sound. The busy ground floor Grill serves hamburgers, sandwiches, and salads for lunch and dinner. The quieter second floor Terrace Restaurant serves dinner only (grilled mahi mahi, shepherd's pie, pasta, grilled filet) against the background of ocean breezes and the twinkling night sky. Wednesdays there is a barbecue with live entertainment. Saturday is usually Mexican night.

The Sand Box (495-9122), a barefoot beach bar at Vixen Point on Prickly Pear Island, is the place to come for an island drink or a great meal. The bar opens at 10 am and they start serving lunch at 11:30. Come here for hamburgers, cheeseburgers, veggieburgers, salads, and sandwiches. At 6:30 pm, they switch to the dinner menu where you'll find conch chowder and pumpkin soup, grilled sirloin steak, sauteed conch, swordfish with a spicy Creole sauce, and grilled Anegada lobster. There's a beautiful little beach and it's an easy hop from The Bitter End Yacht Club or Biras Creek. Tie up at the little dingy dock. There is entertainment Mondays and Wednesdays in season and Wednesday is lobster night. *Closed August to mid-October.*

Saba Rock Resort (495-7711) is on what was once just a spit of a rock. In fact long-time visitors who used to pull their dinghy up to the rickety little dock on old Saba Rock and stop in for a hot dog and a beer or two will not believe their eyes. The sportfishers tied up here are larger than the original bar. In any case this is now a tiny resort and a breezy restaurant. There's a "pub" menu served from noon until 9 pm with cheeseburgers, sandwiches, and Caesar salads. In the evening, there is also a large buffet for $25 or a two-pound lobster plus a salad bar for about twice that amount. To get here for lunch, dinner, or just a drink, catch the water taxi from the Bitter End Yacht Club, which is not much more than a hundred yards away.

NIGHTLIFE ON NORTH SOUND

Schedules change all the time so check local papers or look for a copy of the Limin' Times, *which comes out weekly and is very accurate. It's also a good idea to call before you go.*

The Bitter End Yacht Club usually features live entertainment on Sundays, Wednesdays, and Mondays.

Drake's Anchorage spotlights Ruben Chinnery on Saturday evenings. Head here to listen to Ruben play his guitar and sing a remarkable array of songs.

Pusser's at Leverick Bay has live music on Wednesdays, along with an outdoor barbecue.

GREAT PLACES FOR
PEACEFUL COCKTAILS

Biras Creek. The terrace at the "Castle" here is a spectacularly romantic place to come for sunset cocktails. You can't actually see the sun go into the water but you are high enough to catch the changing colors of the panorama of water, sky, and hills.

Drake's Anchorage has a low-ceilinged cozy bar built of island rock. It's open to the breezes and set right along the water's edge, so you can listen to the lapping waves as you gaze across North Sound, watching the sunlight change to nightlight.

Pusser's Terrace Restaurant has a second-floor bar that is a peaceful spot to drink in the breezes and watch the changing evening light.

NORTH SOUND'S GREAT RESORTS

Along the shores of Virgin Gorda's North Sound are several great places to stay. Three are accessible only by boat. Few places have rooms keys but you can lock yourself in at night, if you wish. If you want to check out the resorts in the Valley on Virgin Gorda, see page 106.

*Rates are **per night for two people** on season (off-season in parentheses), without meals unless otherwise stated, and do not include the 7% government tax or service charge (5%-15%).*

BIRAS CREEK

One of the Caribbean's most romantic and intimate hideaways, Biras Creek is a sophisticated escape, a place to come for superb cuisine, sparkling service, and elegant suites.

Biras Creek is spread out over 140 acres on a peninsula and is accessible only by boat. Suites are in duplex cottages, most of which are tucked here and there along the water's edge. All have very private entrances that are hidden among tropical flowers so you never know you are sharing a building with someone else. These spacious and inviting suites include a comfortable sitting area with a coffee maker and little fridge, a separate bedroom, a delightful garden shower open to the sky, and a large and very private patio. All have both air conditioning and ceiling fans; happily, with either, you can fall asleep to the peaceful sound of the waves. Dinner (see Restaurants, page 113) and drinks are served in the "Castle," a splendid stonework structure set high on a hill with knock-out views of both the surfy Caribbean sea and tranquil North Sound. Guests gather in the open-air lounge and on the terrace for before-dinner drinks and after-dinner, three nights a week, to trip the light fantastic.

This is an incredibly easy place to do nothing or anything. Head to the secluded swimming beach or the spectacular pool overlooking the ocean, explore North Sound in a dingy, play tennis or snooker, ride a bike, hike, be dropped at a deserted beach with a picnic, take a sail to Anegada. Before bed, relax on your patio — the total absence of artificial light makes for extraordinary star gazing. Two Grand Suites feature oversized seaside terraces and sunken baths. Sail-A-Way packages include two nights on a captained private yacht. *33 suites. Rates including meals $750-$850 ($525-$650). Grand suites more. General Manager: Michael and Lu Nijdam. Reservations: 800-223-1108. Tel: 284-494-3555. Fax: 284-494-3557. P.O. Box 54. E-mail: biras@biras.com.*

116

DRAKE'S ANCHORAGE RESORT INN
On this private island there are ten simple rooms and seven beaches. If you want to live in a bathing suit and bare feet, and just slip into a coverup for dellightful meals, then this might be the perfect spot.

Mosquito is a 126 acre, hilly island that lies on the northwest side of North Sound and is home to this tiny, modest resort. Rooms are in three rustic, wood-framed cottages not far from the quiet shore of North Sound. Some have separate sitting areas. All are very simply decorated and have ceiling fans but no air-conditioning. There are also two villas.

The restaurant is right smack on the water and dinner is served with the sound of quiet waves lapping against the shore. Although the island is private, it is not completely isolated. Yachts stop here (there are a dozen moorings) for lunch and dinner and the restaurant and bar can be full of yachties exchanging sea stories. You can spend your days dingying around North Sound in search of the best snorkel spots or you can lie in a hammock outside your room or you can follow the hiking trails to hills and beaches. Rates include meals, unlimited use of windsurfers, snorkel equipment, a 19' sailboat, kayaks, bikes, and dinghies.

Closed July-September. 10 units, 2 villas. Rates (including meals and unlimited use of facilities (see above): $515-$690 ($405-$515), villas more. Tel: 284-494-2254. Fax 617-277-7771. P.O. Box 2510.

THE BITTER END YACHT CLUB
Practically a scheduled stop for charterers (if it's Thursday this must be the Bitter End), this busy marina is a great spot for families and couples who like to sail or who want to learn how and for people who like to spend their days on the water. You can actually stay overnight on one of their sailboats at a mooring, if you want.

Accessible only by water, the Bitter End Yacht Club is nestled along the shore overlooking North Sound and Statia Sound and has 100 moorings. The waterfront area is bustling, with boaters coming ashore for provisions, kids taking sailing lessons, couples heading out on dinghies with a picnic. The Hillside and Beachfront Villas are spacious and peaceful (they're around the hill from all the bustle) and a wide deck, complete with hammock, runs along two sides of each room. The large dressing area includes a little fridge, two sinks, and ample closet room, and there is a separate huge walk-in shower. Hillside rooms are in the trees and the views from bed are great. Rooms are cooled by ceiling fan and are glass top to bottom on two sides (sliding doors

117

and windows, all with screens) and you can lie in bed and watch the sun rise and then fall back asleep. The beaches aren't top notch here but you can dingy to many wonderful ones and there's great snorkeling all over the place. There's also a pool (usually closed September), a fitness trail, and hiking trails. Combination buffet-plus-your-choice-of-entree meals are served in the Clubhouse. The Admiral's Package is the most popular and includes all meals, an introductory sailing course (The Nick Trotter Sailing School is located here), daily excursions, unlimited use of The Bitter End's outstanding fleet of sunfish, lasers, hobie waves, kayaks, and more. You can also stay overnight on a 30' sailboat, even if you have never been on a boat before.

95 units, including 8 "Freedom 30" Yachts. Rates: $585-770 ($400-$550), including breakfast, lunch, and dinner. Admiral's Package (described above) rates for five nights: $3,640-$3920 ($2,240-$2,940). General Manager: Sandra Grasham. Reservations: 800-872-2392. Tel: 284-494-2746. Fax 284-494-4756. P.O. Box 46.

LEVERICK BAY RESORT
The small hillside hotel here is a perfect economical stop if you like water sports and want to spend your days exploring North Sound. You can also rent condos or villas at Leverick Bay through this hotel. Leverick Bay, although tiny, is the largest "settlement" at the north end of Virgin Gorda. It's a steep 25-minute up and down drive from the Valley.

Sit on your balcony here and savor the sight of North Sound at sunset. Simple hotel rooms run along a hillside and the views are terrific at this casual spot. You can also watch the activity at the little dock down below, which is the home of Leverick Bay Watersports, the hub of water activities on North Sound. Stop by to rent a dingy, sign up for day sails, water-ski, or parasail. You can dine at the Pusser's restaurant and shop in several stores. There's a tiny sliver of beach and a small pool.

Leverick Bay is the only place on North Sound where you will find a number of rental villas, from simple cottages to fancy houses. Villas range in size from one to five bedroom and some have swimming pools.

14 rooms. Rates $149 (off-season $119). Call for rates on condos and villas. General Manager: Monica Willis. Reservations: 800-848-7081. Tel: 284-495-7421. Fax 284-495-7367. P.O. Box 63. E-mail: leverick@virginbvi.com.

SOME BESTS OF THE BVI FROM A TO Z

ATMOSPHERE for a romantic dinner: Brandywine Bay
BREAKFAST: Little Dix or the Olde Yard Inn
CINNAMON BUNS: Christine's on Jost Van Dyke
DIVE Site: The Rhone
ENTERTAINMENT: Ruben or Quito or Foxy or O-2
FITNESS TRAIL: Sage Mountain
GIFTS: at any Pusser's Store or Sea Urchin shop
HIDEAWAYS: elegant Biras Creek
ISLANDS: yep, The BVI
JOGGING: Peter Island
KAYACKING: The Bitter End
LEMON TART: at Marlene's in Road Town
MASSAGE: at Fort Recovery or by Cynthia Wilson
NICKEL BEER: Pusser's, of course
OUTDOOR RESTAURANTS: all of them
PAINKILLER PUNCH: Soggy Dollar Bar on Jost
QUIET COCKTAILS: the terrace at Biras Creek
RUM: Pusser's
SNORKELING: the Dogs or the Caves
TENNIS: Long Bay Resort
UNDERWATER VIEWS: everywhere in the BVI
VIEW: Skyworld
WINES: Fort Wine Gourmet
XANTHOUS flowers: Botanical Gardens
YACHT CHARTERS: The Moorings
ZOUK audio cassettes: at Bolo's.

PRACTICAL INFORMATION

Banking
On Tortola, you'll find several banks in Road Town, including Barclay's, Chase, and Scotiabank. There is a branch of Barclay's in the Valley on Virgin Gorda. No other islands in the BVI have banks. Some BVI banks have ATM machines but they are often on the blink, so please don't count on getting cash from them.

Crime
It's rare on Tortola, and exceedingly rare on the other British Virgin Islands. However, there's no point in creating temptation, so don't leave your wallet or your expensive camera lying around.

Currency and Credit Cards
The currency is the U.S. dollar. Most places take credit cards but you will encounter some establishments that take only cash, so bring some cash or traveler's checks. There is no sales tax but is there is a 7% hotel tax and hotels add a 5-12% service charge.

Car Rentals
Cars can be rented on Anegada, Tortola, and Virgin Gorda and run about $50 a day. If you are staying at a resort, you will probably find it easier to get there first and then rent a car. Virtually all car rental agencies will pick you up and some resorts have rental agencies right on the premises.

Documents
You will need a passport to enter the BVI.

Drinking Water
Generally it is good. Larger resorts have their own desalinization plants and make their drinking water. If in doubt, ask.

Getting to and from the BVI
American flies direct from many U.S. cities to Puerto Rico, and connects with American Eagle flights to the little Tortola/Beef Island Airport. You can also fly to St. Thomas from many U.S. cities on American, Continental, Delta, TWA, United Airlines, and U.S. Airways and catch a ferry from downtown St. Thomas to West End or Road Town on Tortola or the Valley in Virgin Gorda. If you are coming from the UK, the best connection is British Airways to Antigua and then LIAT to Beef. Save some money for your return. There is a $10 per person departure tax at the airport ($5 if you are leaving by boat).

Public Holidays

Below are the major BVI holidays. Some float a bit, since they are tied to the moon or to something else that is floating. Banks and virtually all shops will be closed on these days. If a holiday falls on a Sunday, then you can count on the next Monday being a holiday, too. August Festival is actually a two week period of festivities that sometimes begins a little before it officially begins.

> New Years Day: January 1
> Commonwealth Day: 2nd Monday in March
> Good Friday
> Easter Sunday
> Easter Monday
> Whit Monday: floats, late May or early June
> Sovereign's Birthday: June 11th
> Territory Day: July 1st
> Festival: ends with holidays 1st Monday-Wednesday in August
> St Ursula's Day: around October 21st
> Birthday of Heir to the Throne: November 15th
> Christmas Day
> Boxing Day: December 26th

Telephone

The area code for the BVI is 284 (which is easy to remember because it is BVI). When you are in the BVI, use the seven-digit telephone number.

Time

It's Atlantic Standard Time, which is one hour ahead of Eastern Standard Time. However, the BVI does not switch to Daylight Savings Time and during these months the BVI are on the same time as the U.S. eastern time zone.

Weather

Everyone tends to assume that the further south one goes, the hotter it is. Not true! The BVI temperatures hover around 75 degrees in the winter, 85 degrees in the summer and the trade winds almost always blow. New York City can be much hotter in August than the BVI!

What to Bring

Sun screen (the BVI are only 18 degrees from the equator and the sun is strong all year long), a little stick of bug repellant that you can keep in a pocket or purse, casual clothes. In the evening at the nicer restaurants on Tortola and Virgin Gorda, casual elegant resortwear is appropriate, including long pants and collared shirts for men. Only Peter Island and Little Dix require jackets. If you are staying on Jost Van Dyke, Anegada, or Cooper Island then you only need very casual clothes. Bring sturdy shoes if you want to hike and you might want a light sweater as evenings can be cool any time of year.

APPENDIX

FERRY SCHEDULES

BETWEEN TORTOLA AND JOST VAN DYKE

The ferry *When* (494-2997) and *Paradise Express* (495-9477) both take 30 minutes to reach Great Harbor, Jost Van Dyke. The fare each way is $10.

Schedule for the *When*

From West End, Tortola	From Jost Van Dyke
7:30 am (except Sun.)	8:30 am (except Sun.)
9:30 am (Sun. only)	11:00 am
9:45 am (except Sun.)	3:00 pm
1:30 pm	5:00 pm
4:00 pm	

Schedule for the *Paradise Express*

From West End, Tortola	From Jost Van Dyke
7:45 am (except Sat.,Sun.)	7:00 am (except Sat., Sun.)
10:15 am	8:15 am
1:00 pm	12 noon
4:20 pm	3:20 pm
6:00 pm	5:25 pm

Note: Often on-season on weekends or whenever enough people ask, there is a dinner ferry which leaves West End at 6:30 and returns later in the evening. Call if you're interested. Also, sometimes the Nubian Princess *makes the Tortola-JVD run instead of the* When, *and then the ride is only 20 minutes.*

BETWEEN TORTOLA AND COOPER ISLAND

Extremely limited ferry service runs between Cooper Island and Prospect Reef Marina just outside of Road Town, Tortola. Schedules are subject to change, so please call (494-3721 or Prospect Reef 494-3311). Fare is $10 each way.

Mondays

From Cooper	From Prospect Reef
7:00 am	2:30 pm

Wednesdays

From Cooper	From Prospect Reef
7:00 am	11:00 am
3:00 pm	4:00 pm

Fridays

From Cooper	From Prospect Reef
7:00 am	11:00 am

BETWEEN TORTOLA AND VIRGIN GORDA (THE VALLEY)

In Tortola, ferries leave from the ferry docks in Road Town (across from Pusser's). In The Valley, ferries leave from the public dock just north (and within walking distance) of the Virgin Gorda Yacht Harbour. The fare is $10 each way and takes about 35 minutes.

on SPEEDY'S FERRIES (495-5240)

Monday through Saturday

From Virgin Gorda	From Road Town
8:00 am	9:00 am
10:00 am	10:10 am (Tues, Thurs only)
11:30 am	12 noon
2:45 (Tues, Thurs)	1:30 pm
3:30 pm	4:30 pm
	6:15 pm (Tues, Thurs only)

Sunday

From Virgin Gorda	From Road Town
8:00 am	9:00 am
4:30 pm	5:15 pm

on SMITH'S FERRIES (495-4495)

(Daily, unless noted)

From Road Town	From Virgin Gorda
7 am (Mon-Sat)	7:50 am (Mon-Sat)
8:50 am	10:15 am
12:30 pm	2:15 pm (Mon-Fri)
3:15 pm (Mon-Fri)	4:00 pm (Mon-Fri)
4:15 (Sat, Sun)	3:00 pm (Sat-Sun)
	5:00 pm (Sat-Sun)

BETWEEN TORTOLA AND VIRGIN GORDA

The **North Sound Express** (495-2138) runs sleek powerboats between Tortola's east end (at the Beef Island dock, past the airport) and the Bitter End Yacht Club on North Sound. The trip takes 30 minutes (45 if there is a stop at the Valley) and is $40 round trip. From Beef Island, stops can be made at the Valley on Virgin Gorda if requested in advance. Reservations are essential.

From Tortola/Beef Island	From North Sound
8:15 am	6:45 am
11:15 am	9:00 am
1:00 pm	12 noon
3:45 pm	2:45 pm
5:30 pm	4:30 pm
7:30 pm ($25 one way)	6:15 pm (usually)

BETWEEN TORTOLA AND MARINA CAY
The trip takes about 10 minutes and is free. Ferries leave from the little dock near the Trellis Bay Market which is a bit east of the Beef Island airport.

From Beef Island	From Marina Cay
10:30 am	10:15 am
11:30 am	11:15 am
12:30 pm	12:15 pm
3:00 pm	2:45 pm
4:00 pm	3:45 pm
5:00 pm	4:45 pm
6:00 pm	5:45 pm
7:00 pm	6:45 pm
	7:45 pm
	8:45 pm

BETWEEN TORTOLA AND PETER ISLAND
The trip takes about 30 minutes. Ferries leave from the resort's private dock, which many still call the CSY Dock, which is ten minutes outside of Road Town, on the east side of Road Town Harbour. The fare is $15.00 per person. Fares are waived for those who have dinner reservations at Peter Island.

From Road Town	From Peter Island
7:00am	8:00am
8:30am	9:00am
10:00am	11:30am
12 noon	1:30pm
2:00pm	2:30pm
3:30pm	4:30pm
5:30pm	6:00pm
7:00pm	7:30pm
8:00pm	10:00pm
10:30pm	11:30pm

BETWEEN GUN CREEK, VIRGIN GORDA AND THE BITTER END YACHT CLUB (NORTH SOUND, VIRGIN GORDA)
The trip takes about 10 minutes and is free. At Gun Creek, the little wooden Bitter End ferry leaves from the wooden dock. You can grab a beer or a soda from the Last Stop Bar across the street. And don't worry if there's not a soul around or a boat in sight. The ferry will appear! The ferry **leaves Gun Creek every hour on the 1/2 hour** beginning at 6:30 am and ending at 10:30 pm. The ferry **leaves Bitter End every hour on the hour** beginning at 6:00 am and ending at 11:00 pm.

ABOUT THE AUTHOR

Pamela Acheson was Vice-President and Director of Marketing for a Fortune-500 publishing company in New York City until she and her husband headed south over a decade ago. Since their successful escape she has lived in, explored, and written extensively about Florida and the Caribbean.

The Best of the British Virgin Islands, Second Edition is the latest in her "Best" series, which includes *The Best of St. Thomas and St. John, U.S. Virgin Islands,* and, with her husband Richard B. Myers, the award-winning *The Best Romantic Escapes in Florida* and *More of the Best Romantic Escapes in Florida.*

In addition to her own books and consulting, Ms. Acheson regularly contributes to many guide books including *Fodor's Caribbean, Fodor's Virgin Islands, Fodor's Florida, Fodor's Walt Disney World,* and *Fodor's Cruises and Ports of Call.*

Her articles and photographs have appeared in numerous publications including *Travel and Leisure, Caribbean Travel and Life,* and *Florida Travel and Life.* She lives and travels in Florida and the Virgin Islands with her husband.